T0193672

PURPOSE, PASSION & PURSUIT

Enduring the Journey of
Manifesting Destiny

WRITTEN BY
PETER E. DONALDSON

PURPOSE, PASSION & PURSUIT
ENDURING THE JOURNEY OF MANIFESTING DESTINY

iUniverse books may be ordered through booksellers or by contacting:

iUniverse
1663 Liberty Drive
Bloomington, IN 47403
www.iuniverse.com
1-800-Authors (1-800-288-4677)

ISBN: 978-1-5320-1956-2 (sc)
ISBN: 978-1-5320-1957-9 (e)

Library of Congress Control Number: 2017907143

Print information available on the last page.

iUniverse rev. date: 10/03/2017

DEDICATION

The completion of the this book was not obtained without much persistence and determination, as I strived to pick myself back up after each time I stumbled over life's hurdles. Had it not been for the encouraging voice of a loving mother, **Verna Nugent**, I would not have developed the measure of fortitude that I needed to stand and continue to run this race. I am grateful for the favour that God has placed in my life to be blessed to have such a faithful mother. Thank you Mom for your pure heart and for always being an anchor and a shield for me. I love you. It is for this reason that I find it most fitting to dedicate this book to you. It is because you believed in me that I continued to believe in myself.

CONTENTS

ACKNOWLEDGEMENTS

There are numerous individuals who have contributed to the process of my purpose in some way, but there are some specific individuals who stood out significantly. As always, I am grateful for the role that my family and close friends have played in my life, but I would be remiss if I were to forget the mentors and leaders who were divinely placed in my path to help orchestrate my growth. With that in mind, I want to express my gratitude to a few of the spiritual leaders who have made a notable impact on my life.

Firstly, **Pastor Richard J. Brown**, who has continued to be many things to me: A friend, a mentor, and a spiritual covering. I am tremendously grateful to you Sir, for presenting to me an authentic example of what it means to live gracefully and in excellence. I could write a book on the type of man that you are. I respect how you carry yourself in so many aspects of your life, within your family, as a father and a husband. I am inspired by how you lead a large group of people with a manner of simplicity and humility, yet simultaneously motivating those people to achieve progress, while you encourage them to maximize the gifting within them. I would not be where I am today if it wasn't for the grace of God; but surely, I also would not be where I am today without your obedience to the voice of the Lord to become a conduit of grace in the way that you lead. Your graceful leadership has helped to develop my character and you have helped me to become a balanced, more confident, and a more disciplined man. Thank you Pastor Brown. You have made such a positive impact on my life. I am grateful that the Lord has placed you in my life and I am proud to call you my pastor.

Pastor Linford Montague, I am grateful for your guidance during the early stages of my young adult life. You cradled the buried talents of a wandering young man and steered me into the direction of leadership, as you helped me to see the potential within myself. You are a man of humility who demonstrates love through actions of kindness. Thank you for all that you did for me; you helped me to discover the gifts that God has bestowed upon me, and you have assisted in the igniting of great passion that continues to burn vehemently for my purpose. May God continue to bless you, your loving wife, and your entire family.

To the man who God used to usher me into the understanding of salvation, the man who prayed over me as he baptized me at the age of 15 years old, **Pastor Lloyd C. Taylor,** I say thank you Sir. Although Pastor Taylor has gone home to be with the Lord, his legacy of integrity lives on. So many convicting words were preached with such zeal and reverence; he was intentional with his words and I am grateful for the faithfulness in which he presented the gospel of our Lord Jesus Christ.

Elder Ruth Lewis, thank you for your transparency and authenticity. Your prophetic ministry has been significantly influential to the growth of my calling and I am grateful for your ability to often correct, while simultaneously consoling, and doing so with a spirit of love and genuine concern for my well-being. Thank you for helping me to unlock the faucet of my purpose so that the rivers of destiny may flow freely. You are a blessing to my life.

As we continue in this journey of life, trying to balance the spiritual and temporal realities, having mentors within each realm is crucial in arriving at success. We can do many things on our own, but life is lived more efficiently when we are guided by individuals who have already travelled along the roads of our path. With that being said, I would like to express tremendous gratitude to **Principal Lana Cumberbatch**, who has been instrumental in the progress of my career as a teacher in the public school system. It is a blessing to have a mentor who remains excellent in her profession, while continuing to walk in the wisdom of the Lord. Lana, thank you for your patience and faithfulness; your friendship is cherished and appreciated. God bless you.

FOREWORD
By: Pastor Richard J. Brown

**"So teach us to number our days, that we
may gain a heart of wisdom."**
Psalm 90:12

This psalm of Moses is the oldest of the Psalms. Psalm 90 presents the concept of time.

One of the most startling aspects of Moses' life is that, in effect, he ran out of time; that is, he died before entering his destiny, the land of promise. So who better than Moses to offer a prayer about time, or more specifically, about the discouraging reality that human life is all too fragile and short?

In our modern society, much of life is spent at a frantic pace and the average individual exerts endless effort striving to keep up with the many demands placed on them.

From the midst of the scurry, we occasionally lift our heads and pause long enough to wonder, *"Just why am I doing this?"* Is there lasting purpose in what we do, or are we caught on an endless wheel?

When we browse through many of the magazines and self-help books of today, we are fed the deceptive and dangerous idea that our worth and meaning will be found once we finally capture the elusive prize of wealth, fame, or similar significance; and off we race again.

Slowly but surely our strength ebbs, and being exhausted, we collapse in the dust, only to realize that from dust we came and irrevocably, to dust we will return.

Regardless of our individual status, this stark reality behooves each of us to examine this question: *What is the purpose of our life when the spotlight has found its next celebrity?*

As a child, the poem of British Missionary C.T. Studd was often recited in our home:

> *"Only one life, the still small voice gently*
> *pleads for a better choice*
> *Bidding me selfish aims to leave and to*
> *God's holy will to cleave*
> *Only one life, 'twill soon be past,*
> *Only what's done for Christ will last."*

Like never before, I believe it is crucial that we stop wasting time being loyal to systems and lifestyles that have not worked, and refrain from being more loyal to ritual and routine than to progress and purpose.

If you are fortunate to live to be 70 years old you will live approximately 25,567 days. If you are 40 right now, you only have 11,000 days left. My suggestion to you regardless of your age is that you make the rest of your life the best of your life.

In his writing, Purpose Passion and Pursuit, Peter E. Donaldson intelligently and quite eloquently stirs the nest of complacency and challenges us to make the rest the best.

Donaldson begins with the challenge of **Optimizing Your Potential:**

> *"You are worth as much as you think you*
> *are worth.*
> *So why devalue yourself?"*

In chapter five, **Puzzle Pieces,** he explores the concept and understanding of purpose by examining three rudiments, being: 1) Origin, 2) Process, and 3) Time. In this section he brilliantly unfolds the truth that, *"Our purpose has everything to do with God's divine plan and nothing to do with happenstance."*

> "We must therefore learn to be at peace in the season of preparation. A premature entry into any calling or ministry might equate to a premature departure as well"

If you're like me, you're all about obtaining a better, more fulfilled life. If you're looking for the place where you really fit and can be your authentic you, then read on!

As you peruse these pages you will be set on an amazing course of transformation. Like a Gladiator, training for reigning, the process is taking you there. There are opportunities ahead of you; don't quit.

Move forward and make the rest of your life the best of your life by embracing your Purpose, Passion and Pursuit.

Richard J. Brown - Pastor
Kingsway Community Life Centre

INTRODUCTION

It was quite a few years ago, at the age of twenty five, when I was sitting in a church service listening to a sermon. In retrospect, I should say that I was hearing the sermon, but to be frank, I had stopped listening. I remember being overwhelmed by a feeling of frustration and uncertainty. I remember thinking, "What am I doing here?" It was a typical Sunday afternoon, so I knew what I was doing there, I was attending church service as usual; but why? In that moment I realized that my Christianity had become a religious experience rather than a purposeful journey. I remember feeling like I was alone in a room filled with people. The speaker was doing all that he could to present what he believed to be a great message. But as for me, it was falling on deaf ears, because it felt like a regurgitation of shallow words that did very little to address the emptiness I felt inside. But in all fairness to the speaker on that day, my frustration did not rest in the core of his message; the source of my frustration was coming from a void within me. That void was a lack of purpose. I had an idea of what God had called me to do, but I wasn't making my best efforts to maximize the opportunities presented to me in that season. I was focusing on the things around me that weren't going right, instead of taking the appropriate actions to change them. I had changed churches for the second time since becoming a Christian, and I was half-way out the door of that one as well. It was in that frustrating moment that the Lord spoke to me and three impacting words were so powerfully imprinted in my mind. Those words were: *Purpose, Passion,* and *Pursuit.* I took out a blank notebook and I began writing right there in the middle of that service. There was a continuous drive within my spirit to dive deeper into the topic of purpose, mostly because I was searching within myself.

A few weeks went by and I was asked by the youth leader at that time to teach a session to the youth of that congregation. I was given the liberty of speaking on whichever topic was laid upon my heart that I felt would be impacting and relevant to the youth and young adults who would be present at this session. I thought, what better time would I have to expound upon the topic of purpose? I began reviewing the notes I had previously written in my own devotional time and those notes were refined into a seven page document, which I presented one afternoon to a receptive congregation. Those seven pages since then have grown into this book, as I've continued to explore the depths of purpose and what that means in the life of a Christian.

I find it a privilege and a joyous opportunity to be able to share with you my perspective of what it means to be passionately pursuing our purpose in the kingdom. Within these pages you will find practical analogies that are based on biblical reports as well as examples from current events that have been taken either from my personal experiences or the observation of others. For those familiar with my previous publication, this is a contrast, in that it isn't poetic in nature. However, there are a few pieces of poetry that have been inserted throughout the book at the end of some of the chapters. Those poems offer a relevant summary to the ideas presented in each chapter that precedes them. I call them poetic interludes. I hope this will be a blessing to you and I pray that the words of this entire book will be edifying, relevant and life-changing. My desire is that your perspective will be shaped into a more positive view of who you are and what you were called to be. Your life matters. Your life has purpose. You were intricately designed to fulfil a role that no one else on this planet can do better. Let's explore the topic of purpose together. Come with me on a purposeful journey through these pages and let's begin a passionate pursuit of purpose. Our reality is relative. I truly believe that if we can change our perspective, we can change our world.

CHAPTER 1

SILENT SYMPHONY

I'm often overwhelmed by the plethora of "R.I.P" status updates that flood the news feed of various forms of social media. Most often than not, it's usually in reference to a very young individual whose life had been sadly taken away somehow. The caption usually states something along the lines of, "gone too soon." The sobering reality is that the statement is always true, because I just can't seem to ever accept that a young man, who died at nineteen years of age, or sometimes even younger, could possibly have lived out the capacity of his purpose. Whether male or female, the death of any young person is such a devastating occurrence.

So we say such things because that's what the logic of the mind tells us and those are the natural sentiments of the heart: *"Such a shame, that's so sad, it's so tragic to hear about the end of such a young life."* Those are all sincere and warranted expressions of the loss of young lives. I have certainly had my share of mourning, concerning the loss of very young individuals. Indeed it is very tragic. But do you know what's even more tragic than dying young? Dying old without ever living at all. A great author and pastor said it best when he described a life without purpose, *"The greatest tragedy in life is not death, but a life without a purpose."* – Myles Munroe

1

Living a long life outside of purpose is like the beauty of a rose kept in a dark room. It's like the magnificent sound of a harmonious symphony played in the key of silence.

Of course a long life should be desired; but a long life of walking outside of purpose is equivalent to the riches of a wealthy man that has been cast ashore along with him, while he remains stranded on a deserted island. What does it profit him then, to have all the riches in the world, amidst a world where his riches have no value? Such is life when there is untapped potential, unused talent and a life lived outside of the will of the Lord.

CHAPTER 2

OPTIMIZING YOUR POTENTIAL

Along the journey of life, there are a few truths that remain constant. One of those realities is, most often than not, people will typically see you in the light that you project upon yourself. Our reality is therefore determined by our mentality, not theirs. Resolve to stop making duplications of past blunders. You are worth as much as you think you are worth; so why devalue yourself? Items of luxury very rarely get discounted. Have you ever picked up a newspaper and ran across an advertisement that was offering bargain basement pricing for a brand new Bentley automobile? I'm guessing that you have not. This fact remains, when a product of luxury is heavily discounted, it usually means it's either worn out, obsolete, defective or was obtained through illegitimate means. *In contrast*: Have you ever gone into the local mall and noticed a desired item on sale, and walked up to the cash register and demanded to pay more than the shelf value? Probably not. Such is life: If you choose to discount your worth, don't expect others to mark you up. You are the epitome of divine artistry, and in the production of divine creation there are no assembly lines; you are handmade, uniquely designed and orchestrated with purpose. There are no recalls in this establishment and there will be no bargain deals; you are an item of luxurious appetite. *As a disclaimer:* Even when you decide to adopt this mentality, and you begin to walk in the lane of purpose, there will still be times where it seems like you have missed opportunities because people don't think you are worth enough. *But remember this*: In such circumstances, if they pass you up, if the onlookers turn up their nose and scoff at your price tag and pass you by, it probably means that you are simply outside of their capacity. Don't sell out, don't devalue your worth. You are Royalty.

CHAPTER 3

<u>FINDING SERENITY AMIDST YOUR IDENTITY</u>

I've discovered that if one desires to be great… at anything, he must first accept with open arms the perception of being ABNORMAL. Embrace it, welcome it… don't be offended by it. Lay a pillow and rest in the acknowledgment that indeed you are abnormal; and thank God for it, because the description of excellence, in any category, means to exist in a state of distinction. Therefore, you cannot be regular; you cannot fit the mold and you CANNOT BE NORMAL and simultaneously accomplish excellence. That is by definition an oxymoron. Resolve to rise above the propensity to exist in the boxed mentality of those who desire to be normal.

If you're feeling frustrated with your company and you're beginning to become disgusted by the foulness of your social environment, it's probably because you're an eagle mingling in the presence of chickens. If you continue to hang with fowls, you're never going to be able to rise to the realms of excellence. You have to realize that standing out isn't always a bad thing. It is instead a necessary prerequisite to distinction. If you're an eagle… be an eagle; because you would be a terrible chicken. So spread your wings and fly!

He who serves two masters does both masters a great disservice, and leaves himself in a state of confusion and discontent. In this life, you will never fulfill your destiny if you remain at war with yourself. You will never please all people, you will never satisfy the desires of all your friends, and you will never silence the criticism of all your enemies. So, why not save yourself the effort and simply choose one to please? Please God, and rest in His peace, as the noise of all others begins to dissipate. *"A double-minded man is unstable in all his ways."* **(James 1:8 KJV)** *But serenity is found in the heart of he* who is resolved within his identity.

At this juncture, it might be a good time to ask yourself: "Who are you?" Not who others say you are, but rather, who has God designed you to be? In this journey, we will explore that reality, and attempt to shake off the false ideologies that some of us have adopted.

CHAPTER 4

DIAMOND IN THE ROUGH

"Have you not known? Have you not heard? The everlasting God, the LORD, the Creator of the ends of the earth, neither faints nor is weary. His understanding is unsearchable. He gives power to the weak, and to those who have no might He increases strength. Even the youths shall faint and be weary, and the young men shall utterly fall, but those who wait on the LORD shall renew their strength; they shall mount up with wings like eagles, they shall run and not be weary, they shall walk and not faint." (Isaiah 40:28-31 NKJV)

There are times when we endure seasons of doubt in our Christian walk, and we begin to ponder about our purpose and our calling. Somehow, the picture that we see and the picture that God presents don't seem to match up. God shows us who we are in His splendor, perfection, and utter greatness. We still see the picture that displays the many times we stumbled along the way. This picture that we paint is often unflattering and usually quite discouraging. We ask ourselves, "How could this everlasting God, The Ancient of Days, use me for His service?" How can He possibly believe that I, the one who failed him numerous times before, can actually now be propelled into a new dimension, where stability and victory becomes a normal state of existence? In this dimension, we no longer buckle beneath the confines of doubt and fear; instead, we begin to grasp the understanding that God truly has purchased our redemption by the shed blood of Jesus Christ. We can now clearly see that we have become royal, exquisite, joint heirs with Christ Jesus. But even in this dimension, there are moments when we are sometimes still faced with a glimmer of uncertainty. It was during some of those moments that God spoke these words into my spirit:

"Do you not know that I called you even when you had no propriety? It was I that saved you when you had no righteousness of your own. But it was My own seed of righteousness and grace that I planted in you to germinate and bear much fruit. It is this seed that must grow and become fruitful within you. It is for this reason that I will not allow you to die. I will not allow you to abort the gift in you; I shall not stand by and allow you to stagnate that which I have planted on good ground. You are the conduit of the seed of my word. Open your mouth and I will fill it with my words of wisdom. I will clothe you in my anointing and my grace will keep you. My love will surround you and my peace shall possess you. Abide in me and let my words abide in you. How long shall I call and you do not answer? I wait for you to answer your calling and fulfill your purpose. My words are established and settled in heaven. Like a plant flourishes and bears fruit, so you will go forth and bear the fruit of my word. Look not on your own strength. Do not ponder on your own ability. I will impart into you my strength and you will go in the strength of the Lord. Hear me now and be blessed. Arise and take flight in the call I have ordained for your life. There is a diamond in the rough; there is a great man of God within that child of disobedience. There is a great king existing within that slave who is bound by issues and inadequacies. I will make you a new vessel and I will create in you

a clean heart. Your vessel, although once marred, shall now be made whole again. From the midst of the fiery trials, I shall bring you forth as pure gold. Yes, I do see your mistakes and understand what you think of yourself. I saw the many times you had fallen and I've seen your sins and your reproach. I've been aware of your bad habits and your weaknesses. Yet, I still called you; "**…and whom He called, them He also justified: and whom he justified, them he also glorified.**" *(Romans 8:30 KJV)*

So in the midst of your pain, I see a conqueror. I see the man of God within the man of transgression. I'll breathe upon you and you will live again. Your branches shall spring forth and your roots shall be planted along rivers of water, and you will be as a tree of life."

> *"In the midst of the street of it, and on either side of the river, was there the tree of life, which bare twelve manner of fruits, and yielded her fruit every month: and the leaves of the tree were for the healing of the nations." (Revelation 22:2 KJV)*

Now go forth, heal the nations with my words that I will place in your mouth. I will cause rivers to flood where there were deserts. I will cause my light to shine in the darkness of every hopeless situation. I will build sinews upon you, and you shall be whole again. Bone to its bone, flesh to its flesh. For the man that you see, he is a mere shadow of the man that I have called you to be. Unlock the treasure that is laid up in your earthen vessel. Allow me to move in you and be your God. I'm standing at the door of your heart and knocking, waiting to enter and transform your life. Let me in, and I will give you the mind of Christ. I will establish my covenant with you, and I will order your steps in My Word. You know not of your worth, nor of your great potential. But I am the Author and Finisher of your faith. I have made you perfect and according to my image.

> *"So God created man in his own image, in the image of God created He him; male and female created He them." (Genesis 1:27 KJV) ~ "I have said, ye are gods, and all of you are children of The Most High." (Psalm 82:6 KJV)*

I will bring to pass the purpose within you. For you only see a portion of your true destiny. The picture that you see is as if you stared through a dark glass; therefore, only seeing the picture partially. But in the fullness of time, I will manifest my glory through your life and you shall know that I have performed it. My glory shall be revealed in you. Go now in my anointing, and be blessed in the city and in the field. All that your hand shall put forth to do shall be blessed. Only remain in me, and do not waver from my precepts. My blessings are conditional but my words are sure."

> *"If you listen obediently to the Voice of* GOD, *your God, and heartily obey all His commandments that I command you today,* GOD, *your God, will place you on high, high above all the nations of the world. All these blessings will come down on you and spread out beyond you because you have responded to the Voice of* GOD, *your God:*
>
> GOD's *blessing inside the city,* GOD's *blessing in the country;* GOD's *blessing on your children, the crops of your land, the young of your livestock, the calves of your herds, the lambs of your flocks.* GOD's *blessing on your basket and bread bowl;* GOD's *blessing in your coming in,* GOD's *blessing in your going out." (Deut. 28:1-2 MSG)*

CHAPTER 5

<u>PUZZLE PIECES</u>

What is the meaning of life itself? We know what the scientific ideology dictates, but what says you? Why are you here? What is your purpose on this side of life? If life is a journey, where is the destination? If life is a test, then who grades it? If the meaning of life is simply meant to be a mystery, what happens when you can't solve the enigma?

Purpose is the plan of God for our lives; the reason for being, the calling that God has placed on one's life. The concept of Purpose can be understood by analyzing the following three rudiments: Origin, Process and Time. These three fundamentals work together in the big picture of Purpose.

> *"Having made known unto us the mystery of his will, according to his good pleasure which he hath purposed in himself: That in the dispensation of times he might gather in one all things in Christ, both which are in heaven and which are on earth; even in him: In whom also we have obtained an inheritance, being predestined according to the purpose of him who worketh all things after the counsel of his will."*
> *(Eph. 1:9-11 KJV)*

"Who hath saved us, and called us with a holy calling, not according to our works, but according to his own purpose and grace, which was given us in Christ Jesus before the world began." (2 Timothy 1:9 KJV)

But, why at times do we seemingly run in the opposite direction of purpose? It is understood that our flesh is not always subjected to the will of God. In fact, it never is. It is our spirit that willingly serves God. Our flesh is in enmity with God, and is therefore engaged in a war against the spirit. The only way to completely subject ourselves to God is to completely die to our carnal nature. The flesh must die for the spirit to reign within our lives. Knowing this, we die daily in a progressive understanding of the method which God uses to manifest His purpose in our lives. The method is simple, *"He must increase, but I must decrease." (John 3:30 NASB)*

It is in that understanding that the believer is propelled into a new dimension, as he/she is elevated to the realization that it is indeed in God's strength that we now operate. Therefore, because the strength of the Lord is perfected during the times that we are weak, and because we operate by His strength, we should know that we cannot fail. There is no failure in God. We only encounter failure when we step outside of His divine purpose, and walk in our own authority and limited vision.

<u>ORIGIN</u>

Pregnant With Purpose

Your purpose existed in the mind of God even before the foundation of the world. For *"...before he formed you in the belly, he knew you; and before you came out of the womb, he sanctified you..." (Jeremiah 1:5 KJV)*

From this statement, we understand that there must have been a starting point to our purpose. Like life, our purpose has a beginning and therefore, it has a Creator. That Creator is God Himself; He orchestrated the impregnation of your spirit with the divine purpose that is embedded within you. Therefore, there is an origin of your purpose.

The word origin is derived from the Greek word arche, which means: "a beginning," or "the active source."

> *"But we ought always to thank God for you,*
> *brothers loved by the Lord, because from the*
> *beginning God chose you to be saved through*
> *the sanctifying work of the Spirit and through*
> *belief in the truth." (2 Thessalonians 2:13 KJV)*

Therefore, by accepting this fact, we conclude that our purpose has everything to do with God's divine plan, and nothing to do with happenstance; it is imperative that our purpose be revealed to us, not chosen. At times, we attempt to try-out a variety of things in life hoping that by chance, these things will bloom and become successful. We're taught that attaining success is like becoming the beneficiary of "the luck of the draw." But the Word of God doesn't teach us that. It teaches us that success is arrived by a conscious determination to place God's precepts in full pre-eminence over our lives. In so doing, while observing and doing the will of God, all that we put our hands to do, in accordance with the will of God, will be successful.

> *"This book of the law shall not depart out of thy mouth; but thou shalt meditate therein day and night, that thou mayest observe to do according to all that is written therein: for then thou shalt make thy way prosperous, and then thou shalt have good success." (Joshua 1:8 KJV)*

We were made to prosper. The God we serve is a prosperous God. There is no lack or want in Him. There is no failure or defeat in our God. If you can believe and receive that, you're on your way in the journey towards fulfilling your purpose.

> *"The young lions do lack, and suffer hunger: but they that seek the Lord shall not want any good thing." (Psalm 34:10 KJV)*

If God is a perfect God and He has made me in His image, and if God indeed cannot fail and His nature dictates that He must progress and never digress, why do we believe that we even have the right to entertain failure in our lives? I should not, I cannot, and I will not fail, as long as I remain in the vine. For if I remain in the vine of God, perpetual life flows from Him and through Him. And in Him there is only life; so my purpose cannot die, it must live.

PROCESS

So, why do some of us sometimes run in the opposite direction of our purpose? There are various reasons, here are a few: Not knowing our purpose, not accepting our purpose, and being bound by fear.

Being Ignorant Of Purpose

Quite often, some of us become like little children, trying to fix a piece into the masterpiece of a puzzle. Most of us can relate to those infamous Jigsaw puzzles, which many of us may have played with as children. There would be a variety of sizes and pieces to the puzzle, and the task at hand would obviously be to put all the pieces together in the correct order so that the puzzle would paint a picture or tell a story. I believe we sometimes try to mirror this childhood game, and transfer the same behaviour when seeking to paint the picture of our purpose. The problem is, without divine intervention, we can never clearly see where we fit into the puzzle without seeing what the completed work looks like. But the Author, the Finisher, the Creator of life itself, who knows our ways and even knows our end before our beginning, seeks to give us clarity concerning the entire picture.

> *"For now we see through a glass, darkly;*
> *but then face-to-face: now I know in part; but*
> *then shall I know even as also I am known."*
> *(1Corinthians 13:12 KJV)*

I believe that through the Spirit we can understand our purpose; because God will give us an understanding that transcends our carnal perceptions. How many times have you seen a child get frustrated because they have just a few pieces left in the puzzle, yet cannot figure out where to put them? Usually, what ends up happening is that child gets so fed up, in a spirit of anxiety to complete this puzzle, he literally tries to force the final pieces into the slots that seem to be close-fitting, but obviously are not the exact match. This often causes the entire puzzle to break apart, even the pieces that were correctly placed are now pushed out of order and the puzzle is dismantled. That of course equates to an even more frustrated child. For the most part, it's usually not that big of a deal for a 7-year-old child who was just passing time anyway; when he gets tired of manipulating this puzzle, he simply runs to the playground and finds something else to amuse himself with. But what happens when we go through that same episode during our adult stage of life, and we are still trying to fit pieces in areas where they don't belong?

In that case, if the "puzzle" gets dismantled, it isn't as simple as changing games. In the game of life, we really only have one basic goal in playing the game, that is completing the puzzle. You either get the puzzle completed, or you don't. There isn't a middle ground. So it is important that we are not ignorant of our purpose, and that we walk daily with the understanding of who we are and whose we are.

Accepting Our Purpose

It is one thing to know your purpose, but it is another to walk in it. Many times we might be aware of what God has called us to do, but we simply don't accept it because it isn't convenient for us at that given time. If we are honest with ourselves, we can testify that many times we are occupied with our own agendas and our own ambitions; so we walk in the opposite direction of our purpose. But personal ambitions aren't always wrong. I argue that many times those same ambitions are God-instilled. These ambitions need to be framed into order and placed under the priority of God's leading, so that they may be subjected to His agenda, not ours.

> *"Delight yourself also in the Lord, and He shall give you the desires of your heart." (Psalm 37:4 NKJV)*

As Samuel was finally able to recognize the voice of God, and as soon as we decipher the direction that God wishes to take us concerning our purpose, we too must be willing to accept this direction and run with it. Enter into the Sabbath rest of Jesus. No longer wrestle with what is destined to be. He will work in you, and nothing, except you, can hinder His plan for your life. He desires that you should show forth His praise and fulfill the promises He has placed in you. His word is true, His promises are sure, they will not fail. They must come to past in the ordained season of your life.

> ***"For verily I say unto you, till heaven and earth pass, one jot or one tittle shall in no wise pass from the law, till all be fulfilled." (Matthew 5:18 KJV)***

The word that God has spoken to you in your spirit will go before you and do exactly what it has been sent to do; it cannot, and will not fail. Arise now, and answer His call. You are highly favoured and chosen by God, He has placed His seal upon you. Answer this call and step into your purpose.

The Fear Factor:

Another common reason we often don't actualize purpose is the simple reality of being crippled by fear: We may know our purpose, and we may even desire to have our lives submitted to God's leading so that our purpose can be manifested; but we sometimes become stuck in yesterday. We become stuck in the yesterday of our transgressions, the yesterday of our failures, and the yesterday of what others said we would always be.

In biblical reports, we see that Saul knew what this feeling was like. There he stood, by his own words he saw himself as belonging to a place of insignificance, and so he disqualified himself before Samuel even had an opportunity to present him to the people as King.

(1 Samuel 9: 20 NLT) *"And don't worry about those donkeys that were lost three days ago, for they have been found. **And I am here to tell you that you and your family are the focus of all Israel's hopes.**"* These were the words of Samuel as he greeted Saul and attempted to assure him of the great purpose that had been assigned to his life, and the tremendous responsibility he

had before him. In response to this daunting proclamation, Saul replied, *"But I'm only from the tribe of Benjamin, the smallest tribe in Israel, and my family is the least important of all the families of that tribe! Why are you talking like this to me?" (1 Samuel 9:21 NLT)*

But Samuel did something very significant to a young man who thought of himself to be quite the contrary: *"Then Samuel brought Saul and his servant into the hall and placed them at the head of the table, honoring them above the thirty special guests. Samuel then instructed the cook to bring Saul the finest cut of meat, the piece that had been set aside for the guest of honor. So the cook brought in the meat and placed it before Saul. "Go ahead and eat it," Samuel said. "I was saving it for you even before I invited these others!" So Saul ate with Samuel that day.""(1 Samuel 9:22-24 NLT)*

It's so wonderful how God always has a way of elevating us even above the confounding cloud of our insecurity. He places us at the head of the table at times when we don't even believe that we belong at the party to begin with. God has set aside something special for you; no matter where you are coming from, and in spite of your history, you are not insignificant to God. He has a plan for your life and if you let Him, He will see it through until it has been accomplished. But we know that the story did not end there. Even after all of this, Saul would still need some convincing; he not only had to deal with the overwhelming weight and uncertainty that existed within his mind, he would also have to deal with the doubt of others.

"So it was, when he had turned his back to go from Samuel, that God gave him another heart; and all those signs came to pass that day. When they came there to the hill, there was a group of prophets to meet him; then the Spirit of God came upon him, and he prophesied among

them. And it happened, <u>when all who knew him formerly</u> saw that he indeed prophesied among the prophets, that the people said to one another, "What is this that has come upon the son of Kish? Is Saul also among the prophets?" Then a man from there answered and said, "But who is their father?" Therefore it became a proverb: "Is Saul also among the prophets?" And when he had finished prophesying, he went to the high place." (1 Samuel 10: 9-13 NKJV)

It was as if a stage was set, but the audience had no idea that they would be familiar with the main performer. You see, Saul had run into some *homeboys* from around the way. These were the fellows who knew him when none of this was even a thought in Saul's mind. These were the people who knew him before God had changed his heart. These were the people who knew him from *high school* and remembered what a pain in the neck he used to be. These were the people from his childhood who remembered when he got arrested during the 8th grade for stealing those shoes from the mall and was sent to Juvenile jail. These were the people who ...well, you get the picture. Of course Saul didn't do any of those things, but some of us did. We all have some sort of history, and inevitably there will be those individuals who *"knew us when...,"* and they will have a negative report even in the midst of God's grace and favour. They will refuse to see the individual that you have become; they prefer to remember the failure of which you were previously associated: *"Isn't this the same dude that we knew from way back when? Who does he really think he is? I mean, come on; so you're trying to tell me that he's a Christian now?"*

These naysayers have such good memories of your failures, even long after you have forgotten those failures yourself. So they will make statements like: *"What is she really trying to pull off here? We remember when she would always sleep around. Is she really going to look me in my face and try to tell me about Jesus now?"*

I'm sure even one of those comments may seem vaguely familiar. Many of us have heard similar critique when we first attempted to turn our lives around, and turn our faces towards the Lord. But I love what it says in verse 13 from the previous passage: *"And when he had finished prophesying, he went to the high place."* This report makes absolutely no indication that Saul answered his critics in that moment. It simply says that after he had done what the Lord led him to do, Saul left the presence of his critics and went to the high place. Now, I'm aware that in this context the passage which is called "the high place" is to be interpreted as the place of worship, but come with me for a moment and let's consider this text from another perspective: When others are critical of what God is doing through our lives and they become envious of where God is about to take us, let's resolve to not waste any time arguing or defending ourselves against their negative reports. Let us set our eyes on higher ground; let us walk on a higher level than those who wish to bury our future with the dirt of our past. Or even if we take the verse in its most literal term: Saul finished prophesying and then went up to *the high place*...the place of worship; that in itself would be an advisable action to take in the face of critics. When you know that you are in the divine will of the Lord, just do what He told you to do and find yourself in the place of worship. Block out the noise of criticism with the utterance of worship.

But even then, after all of those occurrences of affirmation, Saul's cloud of fear still did not dissipate. After a powerful manifestation of prophecy, Saul was still apprehensive about his purpose and he still had doubts about his calling.

> *"So Samuel brought all the tribes of Israel*
> *before the* Lord, *and the tribe of Benjamin was*
> *chosen by lot. Then he brought each family of the*

*tribe of Benjamin before the LORD, and the family of the Matrites was chosen. And finally Saul son of Kish was chosen from among them. But when they looked for him, he had disappeared! So they asked the LORD, "Where is he?" And the LORD replied, **"He is hiding among the baggage."** So they found him and brought him out, and he stood head and shoulders above anyone else." (1 Samuel 10:20-23 NLT)*

This was Saul's moment of presentation before the people who knew him. He was about to be elevated and presented as their leader, the first King of Israel. This was quite a heavy responsibility; but it was more than the responsibility, Saul was fearful of what the people were about to say. He was fearful of rejection and further criticism. He knew where he came from. He already proclaimed that he believed himself to be insignificant, and that his tribe was among the least of Israel. Therefore, Saul had decided that he was going to take himself out of the race, by hiding at the very moment of his appointment. The fear of rejection outweighed the affirmation that he recently received, and so he crumbled beneath the pressure and resolved to hide himself amongst the baggage.

You and I can certainly attest that at some point in our lives we all had some kind of baggage. Some of us still have quite a bit of baggage to put away, but through God's grace He allows us to carry on, even with all the baggage that we bring with us. But Saul's intention was simple. He probably thought, "Maybe if I can hide beneath all this stuff, all of this baggage, all of the clutter, maybe I'll just get lost beneath all of that, and won't be seen."

But Saul was not alone in this mentality. After all, isn't that what many of us do when we finally reach the doorsteps of our purpose? Don't we too try to hide ourselves amidst the baggage of our past, the baggage of our issues and the baggage of our insecurities? Don't we do as Moses did, and begin to list the many reasons why we are the wrong person for the task? Don't we email God with the subject heading "My Resume of Disqualification," indicating the many reasons why we are not enough, not qualified and not fit for the call due to our baggage? Yes, I think we do. I certainly did that. So in that moment, what we do is self-sabotage the mission; in our mind, going AWOL (absent without official leave) is far less intimidating than facing the denunciation of our peers. So we list all of our faults in attempts to forfeit our qualification, not realizing that we were chosen exactly for that reason. God selected many of us for the very reason that we were NOT qualified, because He will not share His glory with another. He delights in the fact that when He saw us, we had no claim to our own righteousness; that means when He cleans us up, when He elevates us, we will have no one else to glorify but God.

Saul was brought from among the baggage, brought from beneath all the *stuff* that he was hiding under. When he finally stood up, it could be clearly seen that he was head and shoulders above all the rest. As soon as you and I resolve to come up from under the weight of our baggage, and as soon as we learn to stop hiding behind all our stuff; God will lift us to a level that is higher than all the baggage in our life that was being used as camouflage, and He'll clean us up and show us that He has brought us to a higher plane than those of our critics. They won't stop criticizing but He will reveal to us what has always been true, but we never realized it: We were never on their level to begin with. The purpose of God had always been inside of us, but we couldn't see it because we had made a prison for ourselves beneath the baggage. Saul was always head and shoulders above his peers, but he was too busy hanging his head below the weight of insecurities that he hardly even noticed. I imagine that Saul may have thought, *"Who am I that you should be speaking these magnificent things about me?"* He must have wondered, *"Considering that I am among the least, who am I that I should be King?"*

Such is the testimony of many of us. Fear grabs a hold of us when we begin to ponder on the calling on our life, and we resort to proclaiming a plethora of excuses as to why God cannot use us. But really, that's all they are, excuses. We try to make it appear as something else, and we even try to make it appear like we are simply residing in the atmosphere of humility. But the truth is, it's not humility that holds us captive, it is fear.

So instead of trying, we exist in a realm of defeat before the battle even begins. In this stage, many fall beneath an umbrella of false-humility. When you ask some of us about our purpose, sometimes we use the camouflage of humility to say the following: "Well I don't like to brag, and I don't really speak much about my purpose, I just wait on God and watch Him work in my life in due season." Well, all that is fine and dandy; but I believe that life and death proceeds from the little instrument we use that's called a tongue. It is by the power of the tongue that we bring to life the things embedded inside of us, by confessing those things into the atmosphere. It is in this practice that we can see true miracles, as God begins to become tangible in our lives. Fear is now crippled instead of us being crippled by fear. *"God has not given us the spirit of fear, but of power, of Love, and of a sound mind." (2 Timothy 1:7 KJV)*

Therefore, shake yourself from the dust and walk into your purpose. No longer run in the opposite direction; instead, march boldly before the King's table and claim your inheritance: *Because "...in all these things we are more than conquerors through him who loved us." (Romans 8:37 NIV)*

23

Embrace The Process

It is the will of God that we pattern our lives after His express image, who is of course, our Lord and Saviour Jesus Christ.

> *"God, who at various times and in various ways spoke in time past to the fathers by the prophets, has in these last days spoken to us by His Son, whom He has appointed heir of all things, through whom also He made the worlds; who being the brightness of His glory and the express image of His person, and upholding all things by the word of His power, when He had by Himself purged our sins, sat down at the right hand of the Majesty on high..." (Hebrews 1:1-3 NKJV)*

Jesus Christ is the embodiment of God; He is that God who manifested Himself in flesh and dwelt among us. We have no closer access to the divinity of God than through Jesus Christ. He is our intercessor; he is our advocate and our friend.

> *"For the grace of God that brings salvation has appeared to all men. It teaches us to say 'no' to ungodliness and worldly passions, and to live self-controlled, upright and godly lives in this present age, while we wait for the blessed hope, the glorious appearing of our great God and Savior, Jesus Christ." (Titus 2:11-13 NIV)*

Therefore, waiting for "the blessed hope" works patience, as we endure the process of fulfilling our purpose. This text instructs that we should deny ungodliness and all things that work against the holiness of God. That being said, I believe that there can also be an even deeper lesson from this scripture. Again, this scripture speaks about the physical returning of the Lord; and as we wait for it, we watch soberly, seeking to adopt the mind of Christ and live clean lives. But, could "the blessed hope" also require us to yearn for the manifestation of Christ inside of us? Is it possible that this hope within us is almost as splendid as the expectation of Christ to physically return? If that is true, then it would mean that we should strive to be mirror images of Christ Jesus, even in our mortal bodies. Of course, on this side of life we will never be able to completely mirror Christ. The word of the Lord declares, ***"Beloved, now we are children of God; and it has not yet been revealed what we shall be, but we know that when He is revealed, we shall be like Him, for we shall see Him as He is. And everyone who has this hope in Him purifies himself, just as He is pure." (1 John 3:2-3 NKJV)***

So essentially we know that we cannot be *completely* like Christ until He returns in His splendor. But the word tells us that if we have this hope of His return in us, in response, we would strive for purity. But not just a form of godliness, we would strive to attain the same measure of purity as Christ exhibits. Now for some, that might even seem contradicting. But here is the main point to grasp from this, when we possess that blessed hope within us, we will have such a desire. We will have such a passion for God's holy nature that we will fervently and vehemently pursue the righteousness of Christ, even while we dwell in our mortal bodies.

It is from that understanding that as a committed believer, you make it your first priority to daily aspire to run passionately after God's presence and after your purpose, until Christ is indeed formed in you. As a mature believer, you must comprehend that the Christian walk is not a destination; in the sense that you pray and fast until you reach an apex and then you simply stop. Rather, the Christian walk is a perpetual journey that does not cease until the day of Christ's return.

This is why it takes patience to endure the process. The manifestation of your purpose must endure a grueling process in order to properly birth that which God has impregnated within you. It is during that process that we move from stage to stage, from glory to glory, and from strength to strength. In this process, there will be hills and there will most definitely be valleys. But as soldiers of Christ, we must endure it all and press on in this journey. *"You therefore must endure hardship as a good soldier of Jesus Christ." (2 Timothy 2:3 NKJV)*

For in all things, there is a process. Even in nature, we see that both a caterpillar and a tadpole experience a metamorphic change that completely evolves their state of being. Tadpoles endure a very unique process of metamorphosis. Not all species of frogs experience their transformation process within the same duration of time. Because of this, a regular tadpole may take anywhere from a few weeks to a few months before it experiences a metamorphosis into an adult frog. Other species of frogs such as the "Bullfrog" can remain in the infancy stage (as a tadpole) for up to two years. This is interesting to me that although it endures a longer process as a smaller, weaker creature, the end result turns out to be much greater than the other species of frogs.

The bullfrog is larger than that of a regular frog, so it would appear that its process of metamorphosis might be worth the wait. The longer that it remains in the state of a tadpole, the larger it will be when it reaches its stage of maturity.

It is also recorded that the bullfrog is a territorial species, and they are distinct from other types of frogs, and among all frogs they are one of the least hunted by predators. To their predators, bullfrogs exude a detestable savour which is somehow different than that of regular frogs; this gives them somewhat of a protection from some predators. As unpleasant as the comparison may be, as believers, we are also sometimes seemingly left in a state of infancy concerning our purpose, and we wonder when our purpose will be manifested. When? We ask; when will we launch out into the deep and develop into the greatness that we've been called to be? From the analogy of the frog's stages of development, we can appreciate the scripture that teaches us that our ending will be greater than our beginning, if we can only endure the process.

"The glory of this latter temple shall be greater than the former," says the LORD of hosts. "And in this place I will give peace," says the LORD of hosts." (Haggai 2:9 NKJV)

Therefore, we must endure a process in order to produce our purpose; but knowing that our end will be greater than our beginning should make the process a bit easier to bear.

God is perpetually taking you and me through a process so that He may continue to move us to higher heights and deeper depths within Him. He is equipping us to be great warriors. So just remember: If your maturation process seems longer than others, it just might be because God is preparing you for a greater battle. He's shaping you to ensure that you're not as susceptible to defeat as others, because your battlefield may be that much more deadly. He's preparing you for a more intense battleground. He is making you into a militant warrior, and for this to be done, you must endure the process.

Let's consider the other unique creature that also endures the magnificent process of a metamorphosis: The Caterpillar. From the second that the caterpillar breathed its first breath, it began the process of becoming a butterfly. Although it had not blossomed into that final stage of its purpose, the process had already begun for it to be transformed from caterpillar to butterfly. Although the process of transformation is not yet completed, its nature and purpose was already instilled within its biological structure. It is destined to become a butterfly, regardless of what its current state of being would dictate.

It is also important to realize that each stage of that creature's life is equally important as the next. This is similar with the life of the believer. While we endure the process, we ought not to think that it is time being wasted; rather, we are simply being pruned, even trained for a greater purpose. The training is as important as the battle itself. Each stage of life that we endure is relevant, and it is an important part of the process of pursuing our purpose. God sees not just who we are at present day, more so, He focuses on who we will become and who we are becoming, because of His grace and unmerited favour. God desires to propel us into new heights and dimensions that cannot be attained until the process is completed.

The butterfly, which has now changed from the state of a caterpillar, may venture into new experiences, as it can now experience life as a butterfly. Soaring and exploring new dimensions that before were not only unknown, they were also unattainable in its previous state. So once again, the process proved to be well worth the wait.

So we see the transformed butterfly: Same being, yet in a different state. Same creature, but a different manifestation. Same life, but a different stage of living. I believe this mirrors the life of the believer as well.

TIME

The definition of ***time*** is derived from the Greek word *Kairos,* which means, "A fixed or definite period, a season," or "the coming age."

> ***"To everything there is a season and a time to every purpose under heaven." (Ecclesiastes*** **3:1 NKJV)**

Time is the third element that enables our purpose to be actualized. Although our purpose was birthed in the realm of eternity in the womb of God's divine plan, it must be manifested in *time.* As the seasons change and are definite in their order, so is our purpose in relation to time. There is an appointed time for our purpose to be birthed; we must be sensitive to the coaching advice of our midwife, which is the Spirit of God. This is imperative in order to bring forth a healthy birthing of our purpose; jumping ahead too quickly might create a premature ministry, like any premature baby that is at high risk in its new atmosphere. The baby, who is similar to that ministry, simply wasn't given enough time to grow in the womb, and therefore was unprepared to face the realities of life. Sadly, many premature babies die without getting a real chance to experience the life that they were destined for.

We must therefore learn to be at peace in the season of preparation. A premature entry into any calling or ministry might equate to a premature departure as well.

On the other hand, waiting too long to give birth to a child also creates a problem. If a mother has exhausted the time expected for her delivery, the birthing process sometimes has to be forced through surgical methods. If the child stays too long in the womb, there is always the possibility that complications may occur. Sometimes we procrastinate as it relates to doing the will of the Lord in our lives, and the enemy's desire is that when we finally decide that it is now convenient for us to manifest purpose, we would find ourselves delivering a still-born baby. But God will not allow that gift within you to die, as long as you continue to walk in the Spirit and stay connected with The True Vine; so continue to draw life from Him and feed that purpose within you, and allow it to grow until its appointed time of birthing.

Let us consider the Iceberg: In its season, it sinks great ships and stands seemingly indefeasibly floating at sea. Its unmovable presence intimidates the greatest of sailors. Yet, there does come a season, a time when the temperature does change and the ice does crumble to fragmented pieces. This season opens the door for transformation, similar to purpose in the believer's life. The passing ships of destiny that seemed to be hindered by the large icebergs of circumstance are merely temporary situations that are bound to be broken by the element of *time*. It is therefore important to remember that if we remain in the will of God, temporal circumstances can never cancel divine appointments. If God said it, then it must be. It shall come to pass!

> *"Then the Lord replied: Write down the revelation and make it plain on tablets so that a herald may run with it. For the revelation awaits an appointed time; it speaks of the end and will not prove false. Though it linger, wait for it, it will certainly come and will not delay."* *(Habakkuk 2:2-3 NIV)*

Let us not be weary in waiting for our purpose. If we do well, in the right season, in the fullness of time we will reap progress, if we do not give in and buckle to the burden of the process. Do not abort your child; your child is your purpose. Your latter days will be greater than your present, if you only endure the wait. Time will heal your wounds. This duration of healing will also serve as a necessary maturation process for your ministry.

But before we can truly grasp the importance of fulfilling our purpose through the process of time, we must first comprehend that our purpose is locked up and tied up in the identity of Christ. Meaning, we cannot live in an optimal realm of purpose until we unveil the reality of Christ's authority; because without His authority, we have no boldness. Without walking with His keys of redemption, we have no access to the mysteries of God. We must therefore search out His identity before we can find our own.

CHAPTER 6

THE AUTHORITY OF CHRIST

The word *authority* can be defined as: The power to enforce obedience, the right to command, or the privilege of granted access.

> *"Blessed be the God and Father of our Lord Jesus Christ, who hath blessed us with all spiritual blessings in heavenly places in Christ: According as he hath chosen us in him before the foundation of the world, that we should be holy and without blame before him in love: Having predestinated us unto the adoption of children by Jesus Christ to himself, according to the good pleasure of his will." (Ephesians 1: 4 - 5 KJV)*

The plan of God concerning the adoption of the church was manifested through the mediation of Christ. That plan existed before the foundation of the earth. Although the authority of Christ existed in the realms of eternity, it was indeed manifested in the fullness of time. Therefore, it is important to understand that it was only after the *Appointed Time* that Christ stepped into this authority as Mediator. Although He always existed and perpetually exists as "The Alpha and Omega, the Beginning and the Ending," before the foundation of the world, it was only after His purpose was fulfilled by His death, burial and resurrection that the veil of the temple was torn; therefore granting us access to God through His shed blood. That action brought forth the actualization of that element of Christ's authority.

> *"⁵¹Then, behold, the veil of the temple was torn in two from top to bottom; and the earth quaked, and the rocks were split, ⁵² and the graves were opened; and many bodies of the saints who had fallen asleep were raised; ⁵³ and coming out of the graves after His resurrection, they went into the holy city and appeared to many." (Matthew 27:51-53 NKJV)*

The torn veil of the temple, as depicted in *Matthew 27:51*, was symbolic of us stepping out of our previous role as servants and stepping into the privilege of sonship. Although we still serve Him as Master and Lord, our very nature was changed with the acceptance of His adoption and by God's grace He blessed us with His godliness. However, His divine authority had no root of creation; that aspect is eternal. The cross was the unveiling of Christ's authority, not the beginning of it. Because Jesus Christ is the embodiment of the word, and the word existed with God from the very beginning, Jesus is eternal; therefore his authority is eternal.

> *"In the beginning was the Word, and the Word was with God, and the Word was God. He was in the beginning with God. All things were made through Him, and without Him nothing was made that was made. In Him was life, and the life was the light of men. And the light shines in the darkness, and the darkness did not comprehend it." (John 1:1-5 NKJV)*

Further evidence of His authority can be seen when we look at documented testimonies from the life of Christ:

> **"Then they were all amazed and spoke among themselves, saying, "What a word this *is!* For with authority and power He commands the unclean spirits, and they come out."** *(Luke 4:36 NKJV)*

> *"Then he called his twelve disciples together, and gave them power and authority over all devils, and to cure diseases." (Luke 9:1 NKJV)*

> *"What do you want with us, Son of God?" they shouted. "Have you come here to torture us before the appointed time?" (Matthew 8:29 NIV)*

It is important that we highlight the fact that even the demons of hell recognized the divinity of Jesus, as well as the potency of His authority. The demons knew that their time was limited. They also understood that while Jesus indeed had the authority to inflict torture upon them, there was an *"APPOINTED TIME"* when Christ would step into the full unveiling of His authority. The demons concluded that this "Appointed Time" had not yet come.

> *"And what is the exceeding greatness of his power to us-ward who believe, according to the working of his mighty power, which he wrought in Christ, when he raised him from the dead, and set him at his own right hand in the heavenly places, far above all principality, and power, and might, and dominion, and every name that is named, not only in this world, but also in that which is to come: And hath put all*

things under his feet, and gave him to be the head over all things to the church, which is his body, the Fullness of him that filleth all in all." (Ephesians 1:19-23 KJV)

The word "wrought" is found in Ephesians 1:20, also meaning "worked," is defined by Merriam-Webster Dictionary in the following manner: *"Carefully formed or worked into shape; worked into shape by artistry or effort."*

Therefore, until **The Fullness of Time** had come, we did not have direct access to the grace of God as we do now. It was only after the adoption through His son that we also became joint heirs with Christ. In other words, although the role of Christ as mediator had a beginning, this did not nullify the eternal deity of Christ.

His role of mediation had a beginning, but His divine identity is eternal. The fullness of Christ's authority existed in eternity but was manifested in time. Although the birth and crucifixion of Christ were both events that occurred on specific dates on a temporal timeline at some point in history, His origin is eternal; His purpose existed before the foundation of the world, and His identity is divine.

"Jesus said to them, "Most assuredly, I say to you, before Abraham was, I AM."" (John 8:58 NKJV)

Here, Jesus very unequivocally settles the matter concerning his divinity, and He declares that before Abraham gave up his last breath and became history, Jesus was already present. *"He is the image of the invisible God, the firstborn over all creation. For by Him all things were created that are in heaven and that are on earth, visible and invisible, whether thrones or dominions or principalities or powers. All things were created through Him and for Him. And He is before all things, and in Him all things* consist. *And He is the head of the body, the church, who is the* **beginning, the firstborn from the dead, that in all things He may** **have the pre-eminence." (Colossians 1:15-18 NKJV)**

> *"For in Him dwells all the fullness of the* **Godhead bodily; and you are complete in Him,** **who is the head of all principality and power."** **(Colossians 2:9-10 NKJV)**

All of this becomes even more relevant when we consider the journey of our own purpose. We are who God says we are, and we are that right now. God has already placed our identity inside of us from before the foundation of the world, but even though that remains true, we still have a process to endure. We are still under the subjection of time.

We must therefore purposefully walk out the plan of God for our lives and submit to His leading. We must embrace His will for our lives as we clothe ourselves in the custom fit tailoring of our purpose.

"And when I saw Him, I fell at His feet as dead. But He laid *His right hand on me, saying to me,* **"Do not be afraid; I am the** **First and the Last. I am He who lives, and was dead, and behold,** **I am alive forevermore. Amen. And I have the keys of Hades** **and of Death.""** *(Revelation 1:17-18 NKJV)*

We have a responsibility to fulfil our purpose. We each have a job to do, and we will be rewarded according to the measure of our production, the content of our character, and the sincerity of our hearts.

> *"And behold, I am coming quickly, and My* **reward is with Me, to give to every one according** **to his work.** [13] **I am the Alpha and the Omega, the** **Beginning and the End, the First and the Last."** **(Revelation 22:11-13 NKJV)**

CHAPTER 7

THE JOSHUA GENERATION

I am of the opinion that the Lord has raised up a generation that will do more than simply "have church" as usual. I believe that this generation is seeking for more than ceremonial routine, and we are on a quest of the tangible manifestation of the glory of God. I believe that this generation will lay aside promiscuity, grab hold of the promise, and step into their purpose. This is the generation that will shun religiosity and pursue relationship with Christ.

This is the generation that will step outside the parameters of their church walls, step into their communities and declare the word of the Lord. They will move forward and set free those who are bound in sin and who remain captive in their minds. This is the generation that will march boldly into the courthouses with authority, and challenge governmental laws and policies that are contrary to the word of God, and declare what "thus says the Lord" in this season. **"And from the days of John the Baptist until now the kingdom of heaven suffers violence, and the violent take it by force.** *(Matthew 11:12 NKJV)*

I believe that God has raised up this generation to participate in an intense battle against the devil, to reclaim the Kingdom for the glory of God. We have a mandate to fight for his kingdom; because *"the earth is the Lord's, and all its fullness, the world and those who dwell therein." (Psalm 24:1 NKJV)*

But somewhere along the journey, the church forgot that this world belongs to God. Somewhere amidst the fight, we forgot that we've already won the war; all we have to do is allow God to conquer each battle through us. But the war is as good as over. It's finished! So why then do we continue to run around in circles, wandering away from our purpose? This is the Joshua generation. Joshua arise, shake yourself from the dust and step into the promise land and claim the land which God has already given to us.

Joshua: *"Arise, shine, for the light has come, and the glory of the Lord is risen upon you." (Isaiah 60:1 NKJV)*

CHAPTER 8

<u>PURPOSE REVEALED</u>

You were bleeding when He first called you, filled with the wounds of sin. These wounds have been healed and wounded again, and again. Yet, God is still the same now as He was then. His grace is more than enough to deliver us from the crippling effect of sin and fear. His heart longs to be with you in perpetual communion. It's only in this place of communion, this secret place, that He speaks to us in clarity and directs us towards our purpose. It is there in that secret place that He reveals to you unseen mysteries.

Let Him give you an anointing like you've never before received. He knew you were going to falter along the way. He knew you would slip from time to time; yet He still called you and He still bestowed His grace on you. Even though you've strayed from purpose so many times, He's already planted in you all that you need to win.

Now is the time that you should arise, get up from your past and present mess. Step into the blessings of your future and cultivate the seed within you! Take control over your mind, your emotions and your carnal habits. He has created you for such a time as this; there is great purpose for your life. Trust in Him and allow Him to lead. He will not leave you comfortless. He will not render to you what you deserve; had He judged you and me in the measure that we deserved, we would not be able to stand. Yet, God has granted us grace and favour in His sight. God's grace goes far beyond the cross. His favour runs deeper than the balance in your bank account. The Lord will **"keep *you* as the apple of the eye and hide *you* under the shadow of *His* wings." (Psalm 17:8 KJV).**

He will not allow you to die. Your gift, your ministry, and your life, all of these things are too valuable. The purpose within you has been instilled as an investment by the Lord. God, like all good investors do, expects an abundant return on His investment. No one invests in hopes of just breaking even. All investors desire increase; God is no different. Similar to the Stock Market, that from time to time goes through its rises and falls, its bumps and potholes, you also have gone through some inconsistencies in your journey. But the progression from mountain to valley, to mountain again, is absolutely necessary in our journey towards the land of promise. It's just simply a part of the geographical structure. Life has hills and valleys, there is very little we can do as it relates to that fact.

But even during those moments when you feel like you are indeed on spiritual life-support and you begin to watch the pulse of your heart rate go up and down, just remember, regardless of what things look like around you, you must resolve within your own mind to embrace this mentality amidst life's trials: In spite of what you feel like, you will not, you shall not, you cannot die!

Such a militant philosophy seems illogical to some, and perhaps it is, but when has faith ever been logical? God has locked in *purpose* in your life. He has impregnated your spirit with destiny. It is now the acceptable time to manifest that purpose. It is now time to give birth to your destiny. You will live and not die. You will not crumble beneath the pressure that comes from those who desire your demise.

**"But you belong to God, my dear children.
You have already won a victory over those
people, because the Spirit who lives in you is
greater than the spirit who lives in the world."**
(1 John 4:4 NLT)

It is a reality that the road ahead may at times get dark and
the journey will sometimes seem endless, but hold on my friend,
hold on to God's unchanging hands. Hold on to His promises; hold
on to the words that He has spoken to you. The Word of the Lord
teaches us that we are *more than conquerors.* Well, if a conqueror
is one who is victorious, one who acquires control of his enemies
by force, and we are described as being even more than that, how
confident should we be walking in the lane of our purpose?

*"But now, this is what the LORD says—he
who created you, O Jacob, he who formed you,
O Israel: Fear not, for I have redeemed you; I
have summoned you by name; you are mine.
When you pass through the waters, I will be with
you; and when you pass through the rivers, they
will not sweep over you. When you walk through
the fire, you will not be burned; the flames will
not set you ablaze; for I am the LORD, your God,
the Holy One of Israel, your Saviour..." (Isaiah
43:1-3 NIV)*

MANIFESTING PURPOSE

Until we find a hope that's new,
A hope that gives life, a hope that's true
Until we find a meaning for life itself,
We'll forever store away our purpose on a shelf.

Until money is no longer an object, we'll work each day just to live.
But even with an abundance of wealth, what is
life, if no pleasure of purpose it gives?
For life without purpose is incongruous; like
an oxymoron, very contradictive.
For having a lack of purpose hinders life like a spiritual contraceptive

For where there is no vision there is stagnation and eventually death.
And so we hold on to whatever glimmer of hope is left.
This hope, found not by might, nor by power; but
it's by The Almighty will we discover.
Hoping that through faith, we'll find determination
and that our strength we'll recover.

Rejuvenated strength for the journey, strength
for the battle, strength for tomorrow.
For in times past we wallowed in a realm of defeat,
a realm of pity, a dungeon of sorrow.
Purpose was far from our hearts and minds,
uncultivated seed in a land that was fallow
But great destiny exits in you and me; launch out in
the deep, no longer remain amidst the shallow.

The manifestation of purpose and destiny awaits you now
If you'll only submit and in humility you would bow
Yield to a Maker who is greater than thou
Arise from inertia and fulfill destiny; manifested
purpose on you He'll endow

CHAPTER 9

BEYOND THE SHADOW OF DEATH

The word of God teaches us that although at times we may walk in the midst of darkness that is likened unto death, we should not fear; because the Lord remains with us as a guide and continues to comfort us during those situations. But what do you do when it seems like God has forgotten you? What do you do when it appears as if you have gone even beyond the very shadow of death and God has yet to make an appearance? You've prayed and you've cried; you've fasted and you've declared and affirmed His Word. Yet, sometimes you might still find yourself in a place where it seems like death has come upon you. The pangs of depression grab a hold of your mind. The darts of fear attack your faith and the detours of bad circumstances have left you wondering: Where are you God? Where were you when I felt like I was hanging on by my last thread? Where were you when the spouse walked out, when the mortgage foreclosed? Where were you God when the camouflaged smile on my face was really a front, with hopes of covering the thoughts of suicide in my mind? Where were you God when I questioned my purpose and even my salvation, wondering if you had totally left my presence? God! Oh God, where were you when I felt like I had gone beyond the shadow of death?

Martha and Mary might have shared some similar questions when they watched their dear brother become ill and eventually die.

> *"Now a certain man was sick, named Lazarus, of Bethany, the town of Mary and her sister Martha it was that Mary which anointed the Lord with ointment, and wiped his feet with her hair, whose brother Lazarus was sick. Therefore his sisters sent unto him, saying, Lord, behold, he whom thou loveth is sick. When Jesus heard that, he said, this sickness is not unto death, but for the glory of God, that the Son of God might be glorified thereby." (John 11:1-4 KJV)*

Here we have Lazarus, the brother of Martha and Mary; the brother of the woman who poured out her heart and soul to Jesus. This was the woman who went beyond the protocol of a legalistic society and unveiled her hair, washed Jesus' feet and wept before Him. It was this same Mary, whom Jesus loved, who was now facing a desperate need. It was this same Mary who worshipped before the Lord without reserve. In this medical predicament, if no one else was deserving of a visit, surely, Mary was; the Lord would not allow her brother to die. Surely he would come to the need of Lazarus and help this family, of whom it was said that Jesus loved. If for no other family, the Lord would definitely respond to this one, and make his appearance before death would have its way and make this situation impossible to recover... wouldn't he?

> *"Jesus loved Martha and her sister and Lazarus. Yet when he heard that Lazarus was sick, he stayed where he was two more days. Then he said to his disciples: Let us go back to Judea." (John 11:5-7 NIV)*

Have you ever felt like God has heard your cry, knows the pain that you endure and yet remains still, folds His hands and seemingly does nothing? Has God ever delayed so long that the situation had become detrimental? Yet, God whispers within your spirit and simply says, "Be still."

Well, Jesus does just that. Lazarus is sick; Jesus has heard the news and decides to take a rest, seemingly unconcerned with Lazarus' demise. However, He did respond; I imagine that Jesus did so in a rather nonchalant manner as He says, ***"This sickness is not unto death..." (John 11:4 KJV)***

At last, He answers and gives assurance that Lazarus would not die. Anyone hearing this must have breathed a sigh of relief in this desperate situation. It just didn't make sense that Jesus, the Alpha and Omega, the Living Word, would sit back and let this man die; no, of course not. Not our God, not the Rock of Ages, not the I Am That I Am. Yet, in the midst of such assurance, after the proclamation of the words of Jesus, which are sure and does not change, Lazarus dies! The breath of life had gone out of his body and Lazarus goes beyond the shadow of death.

After two days of silence and perceived indifference, Jesus gets up and decides to begin His journey to visit Lazarus after two whole days of hopelessness had already passed. It is here that Martha meets Him along the way. Martha makes a very emotional, yet very logical statement that many of us might have echoed: *"God, had you only shown up earlier, I wouldn't have had to endure this pain, I wouldn't have had to experience the suffering. You could have saved me from the fire; you could have lifted me from the flood."*

Of course Martha did not say all of that to Jesus. Instead, in her dismay, her first response was simply: ***"...Lord, if you had been here, my brother would not have died..." (John 11:21 NKJV)***

Yet, in scripture we see many instances where God didn't save His people from the predicament, but rather, He delivered them through or out of the dilemma. He brought us to it, to bring us through it.

Jesus presents words of encouragement, telling Martha that her brother will live again. Martha, now trying to salvage what little faith she might have had left, expresses concurrence; but Martha had now stooped into a state of what I call rational faith.

*Martha therefore responds to Jesus and says, **"I know that he shall rise again...in the resurrection at the last day" (John 11:24 NKJV)***

Jesus spoke of that present day when He stated that Lazarus would live again; but Martha had now placed Jesus within a mental box of limitations and boundaries. God can never be confined by our boundaries. He is a limitless God existing beyond the borders of our practicality, earthly logic, or carnal perceptions. Martha had all confidence in the resurrection. But like some of us, Martha only believed God in theory; she had completely lost all hope of seeing Lazarus in this life and made reference to the resurrection on "the last day." Martha's faith was somewhat fickle, as she bounces between two opinions. First she states, **"But even now I know that whatever you ask of God, God will give you." (John 11:22 NKJV)**

Yet when Jesus offers hope, Martha can't seem to see beyond the death of Lazarus; knowing that all logical thinking and normative understanding would dictate that death was the final stage. There was no tomorrow for Lazarus. The only faith she had was that, yes, in the last day he who believed in the promise would rise again. Like Martha, at times we slip into a distant, rational faith instead of a "now faith." If God is able then, He is able now!

It takes a supernatural faith to believe in the impossible. It takes an illogical, unconventional faith to believe God beyond the shadows of death; to be in the shadows of death means to exist in a realm where your situation is just a resemblance, or a mere projection of death. Death, at that point, has not taken its final stab. But what happens when you've stepped passed the shadows, and found that you've fallen so far that it appears that you have been buried under the irrevocability of a defunct reality? Jesus answers this question very unequivocally: **"I am the resurrection, and the life: he that believeth in me, though he were dead, yet shall he live." (John 11:25 KJV)**

In our everyday lives, like Mary and Martha, we wonder if the Lord is actually concerned about the confusion that's going on within and around us. Furthermore, during those seasons of delay, during those days when it appears as if Jesus is asleep and unaware of our turmoil, we sometimes aren't comforted by the simple words, "be still." Sometimes, being still is the last thing we want to do. We want the problem resolved right now. We want the immediate restoration of our faith. Before we can totally believe, we often want to see tangible evidence that God will resurrect our dead situation and breathe life into us again. In some instances, that assurance doesn't come when we want it; in fact, most of the times it does not. However, it is at the brink of our redemption that God sets a stage for His glory to be manifested.

> *"The hand of the LORD was on me, and he brought me out by the Spirit of the LORD and set me in the middle of a valley; it was full of bones... Therefore prophesy and say to them: 'This is what the Sovereign LORD says: My people, I am going to open your graves and bring you up from them; I will bring you back to the land of Israel. Then you, my people, will know that I am the LORD, when I open your graves and bring you up from them.'" (Ezekiel 37:1, 12-13 NIV)*

Here God speaks to Ezekiel about the condition of the people of Israel who were in exile because of the hand of Nebuchadnezzar. Many of the Israelites were now scattered abroad and living in a strange land. It can be presumed that this produced a state of hopelessness in the hearts of the people of Israel. So God shines a light of hope in the direction of His people. He brings Ezekiel by the Spirit into a valley, the Valley of Dry Bones, so that God may reveal His plan of redemption for Israel. It would appear that at the dawn of our deliverance, God often gathers an audience so that He may demonstrate that He is exceedingly greater than our circumstances. God speaks to Ezekiel and reveals, that it is by His hand that the children of Israel would be revived. It is by the hand of God that death would be transformed into life. By the contrivance of suffering and hardship, God is still able to bring forth a positive result out of a negative reality. He is still able to resurrect dry bones and breathe life into them today.

In like manner, the situation of Mary and Martha was quite intriguing; the stage was set at the sepulchre of Lazarus. *It has now been four days since the death of Lazarus and it became apparent that Jesus was taking no pleasure in the suffering of these people. Jesus expresses sorrow as He mourns alongside with Mary, the sister of Lazarus. It is during this time that the word of God records a very powerful moment by the use of only two words: "Jesus wept." (John 11:35 KJV)*

The Incarnate Word, the Bread of Life, the King of kings and Lord of lords, wept!

The expressive emotion of Jesus demonstrated that He was sensitive to the hurt and dismay of those around Him, as He still is today. Jesus wants to heal your brokenness; He wants to plug every crevice of your heart and illuminate every dark area of your life.

One of the attributes that separated Jesus from any other well-wisher was that, unlike others, He didn't just show up to offer moral support. Jesus made His appearance in order to bring life, both literally and spiritually. Jesus shows up and straightway approaches the tomb of Lazarus, and while disregarding the religious babble of those around him, He calls for the removal of the stone that confined the callous body of Lazarus.

"But this just doesn't make sense, it has now been four days since the man's death," some might have said. "Surely, he's already dead, what more can be done?" But Jesus reassures Martha that there is no impossibility where God is present. Jesus says: **"Did I not tell you that if you believed, you would see the glory of God?" (John 11:40 NIV)**

So the people relinquish the protest and finally they take away the stone from Lazarus' sepulchre. After praying, Jesus calls forth Lazarus as intrepidly as one who beckons a friend from a momentary snooze: "Lazarus, come forth!" (John 11:43). Immediately, life is restored. By the spoken word of *the Resurrection and the Life,* Lazarus is breathing again! Suddenly the decomposing process is reserved and the rhythm of the heartbeat has been restored. His arteries were now gushing with the flow of blood to and fro within his body. Lazarus was alive again! Lazarus had been brought back to life from beyond the shadows of death! **"O death, where is thy sting, O grave, where is thy victory?"** *(1Corinthians 15:55 KJV)*

Even the very devout man of God we know as Job was not exempt; he also went beyond the shadow of death. He watched his daughters, his sons, his finances, and his social influence, all die. His marriage was walking in the midst of the shadow of death; all hell seemed to have broken loose. But Job was faithful and did not sin against God. Even though Job existed amongst a dead situation, he held on to the only hope he had, God. Therefore, Job boldly declares, *"For I know that my Redeemer lives, and He shall stand at last on the earth."* **(Job 19:25 NKJV)**

No matter what else has died, as long as we can remember that Jesus lives, all hope is not lost. The Lord will strengthen those dilapidated areas of your life, and He's also able to resurrect those dreams and goals that were trampled on and thrown out during the battles of life. He will revive that vision within you that has been resting dormant, while hanging on solely by the life support of His grace. We know this to be true because in the end, after

Job endured his affliction, the Lord blessed him exceedingly. His finances were restored, he was blessed with more children, and it can be presumed that his social influence was also restored. God now vindicated him by demonstrating His never failing grace.

Jonah is a perfect example of God's grace keeping our purpose on life support. Jonah disobeyed God and as result had slipped into a state of spiritual death. Jonah was at a crossroads between revelation and rebellion; he initially chose the road of rebellion. But this detour had done more than simply steer Jonah off course; it almost cost Jonah his life, and almost caused him to abort his purpose in the process. He had not yet grasped the full essence of grace, which God wanted to outpour. He surely understood the concept of judgement. Oh yes, Jonah was ready and willing to be the instrument of judgement. But God wanted Jonah to obey Him. God desired not only to bring salvation to a backslidden people, but also to enlighten Jonah with the demonstration of the power of grace. God's Word is sure; therefore, to step outside of His plan ultimately brings death. Nevertheless, in His favour there is life, abundant life.

But if you've found yourself in a place of darkness, a place of doom and gloom, a place where it seems like all hope is absolutely gone, there is a place in the shadow of death that causes one to look up for divine strength. In that place, you and I may echo the words of Paul: ***"I have been crucified with Christ and I no longer live, but Christ lives in me. The life I live in the body, I live by faith in the Son of God, who loved me and gave himself for me."*** ***(Galatians 2:20 NKJV)***

It's almost as if there is transference of life. In fact, that's exactly what occurs. Beyond the shadow of death, out of necessity, we begin to live through Christ. It is here that we can comprehend Paul's plea for us to die daily. Considering that perspective, it is then easy to understand why I must decrease and God must increase; it's because all life flows through God. Through this truth we see how indeed His strength is perfected even in the midst of our weakness.

The secular world in attempts to create morbid entertainment often uses tools derived from the realm of the occult to help paint fictional characters that defy conventional norms. The film producers create characters such as "the walking dead" or "zombies," as they call them. These creatures are said to roam about the world as the living dead, empty and void, possessing no soul; whose sole purpose is literally to walk about and torment and feed upon the living. Of course, as believers, we shouldn't entertain ourselves with such nonsense and by no means is this analogy what Paul intended for us to draw from his statement in *Galatians 2:20.*

But in a much purer sense, on the spiritual side of things, we do in essence become creatures that could be described as, well..."the living dead."

Except, this description is in no shape or form associated with the occult. It's merely painting a dramatic picture for us to comprehend this aspect of biblical truth. If I must "die daily" as Paul suggests, it stands to reason that the question would be asked, "Who then lives in my stead?" It's quite rational to ask, "For what purpose do I exist, if my duty is to die daily?"

But it's only when we begin to comprehend the statement, ***"For in him we live, and move, and have our being..." (Acts 17:28 KJV),*** that we can see the Christian perspective of the "living dead;" *it is Christ-centered*, not self-centered. Such a perspective is full of destiny and purpose; it breathes submission in its totality. This perspective personifies humility in its true definition. It is a total abandon of selfish motives and agendas, and a prioritizing that places the will of God above all that we esteem to accomplish.

"There is no greater love than to lay down one's life for one's friends." (John 15:13 NLT) This is what Christ did; He laid down his life so that you and I may live through Him. He is the resurrection and the life, the author and finisher of our faith.

A well-known poem called "Footprints," is a wonderful proclamation that shows how in the moments of turmoil, during the storms of life, God steps in and carries us through. He sits on the flood and keeps watch over us. He does this to ensure that the floods do not overwhelm us. He steps right into the fiery furnaces of our lives and becomes our advocate. He prevents the flames from consuming us as it simultaneously burns out sin and dross from our lives. What an awesome God we serve! He does this while enabling the flames to create the image that He, the Potter, has ordained for us to be. Because God himself is indeed a consuming fire, He regulates how much of the flames we are exposed to; because He knows how much we can bear. Aren't you glad God regulates the heat in those fiery trials?

CHAPTER 10

<u>REMOVE THE SHACKLES</u>

Sometimes God has to allow your situation to die in order to resurrect His purpose within you. But when He does resurrect you, He'll do it in such a way that you will have no one else to glorify...but God.

They isolated you because of the terminal sickness of your circumstance. They bound you with the finality of judgment, and placed you in a tomb appropriate for dead things. They buried you with the heavy stones of burden, guilt, shame and the impossibility of redemption. But when God steps in...all dead things must come to life!

It is He who liberates you from the tomb; it is He who commands the rolling away of burdensome stones. But it is YOU, Dear Church, who will have to untangle that man and allow him to change his clothes. Don't become so accustomed to the atmosphere of dead things that you stop believing in deliverance. When God frees someone from a dead situation, don't just stand around staring in disbelief. Instead, act quickly in restoring this individual and remove the dead things from his presence. He won't be able to walk into the newness of his resurrection if you, Dear Church, are unwilling to socially liberate him by the renewing of YOUR mind. You cannot wait until the moment of your comfort to mirror the acts of grace, which has already been exhibited by Christ himself. *"Jesus replied, "I tell you the truth, everyone who sins is a slave of sin. A slave is not a permanent member of the family, but a son is part of the family forever. So if the Son sets you free, you are truly free..." (John 8:34-36 NLT)*

> *"And he who had died came out bound hand and foot with graveclothes, and his face was wrapped with a cloth. Jesus said to them, "Loose him, and let him go."" (John 11:44 NKJV)*

Jesus spoke to Lazarus and commanded him to come forth; come forth from the dead situation in which he once existed. Come forth, come alive, and live again! Then Jesus spoke to the PEOPLE and told THEM to untie him, and to remove his dead clothes, because it was they who had bound him in the first place. Lazarus' sickness brought him to the grave; but after Jesus had resurrected him, it was the chains of bondage imposed by his peers that were preventing him from walking forward.

His hands and feet, BOUND! So although now resurrected, how can he walk towards the direction of his purpose?

His face and head, BOUND! Wrapped in the garment of dead things. So how can he see clearly to perceive the vision of newness that God has bestowed?

We hold a responsibility of ensuring that our brethren do not remain in dead apparel when God has lifted them from the presence of dead things. Don't become more comfortable with morbid realities than of miraculous expressions of redemption.

> *"Dear brothers and sisters, if another believer is overcome by some sin, you who are godly should gently and humbly help that person back onto the right path. And be careful not to fall into the same temptation yourself. (Galatians 6:1 NLT)*

TREASURE CHEST

So you say you've fallen from grace, and now you exist in a realm of sorrow.

So you've fallen yet again, lost your heavenly friend, and now there's seemingly no hope for tomorrow. There's no light at the end of the tunnel, you've lost your anointing, lost your power.

But this isn't what the Lord says; for He's standing at the door of your heart, waiting for you to open and embark on a brand new start, and from sin depart. He is waiting to shine a light in your dark tunnel; words of wisdom he longs to impart. He has bestowed upon you so many gifts and ministries within, but you've turned away and to a life of sin you stray, and so did the confusion begin. But I tell you I've been where you are; you haven't gone too far, there is deliverance from sin.

I haven't walked down the same alley, haven't encountered the same pain. Haven't lived your life, haven't dealt with the same measure of strife, so from judgment I restrain. But this one thing I know is that through it all, it was the love of God that caused me to remain. It was the mercy of Christ that allowed me to cope with the pain I bore.

It was His grace that covered me and took away the hurt I could no longer ignore

This same grace cries out to you, will you answer the call? Please do, to you I implore.

Great mysteries are locked up in you; you are a treasure chest of destiny. But only you hold the keys, the only access is your bended knees, seeking His itinerary

In prayer He'll meet you and mend that broken heart; in Him you'll find your true identity. This lost treasure is yours to discover, time waits for no man. This new path that you'll take will erase all your mistakes and reveal to you His plan. For you'll now walk hand in hand fulfilling your destiny. The Lord will give you the grace to stand.

CHAPTER 11

GIDEON'S PLIGHT

Gideon's dilemma was that he was called to do a task that was seemingly impossible. In fact, all mathematical and practical calculations would determine that his task was not possible. Not only was Gideon seeing himself as a "nobody," he also now had to believe that this nobody had been chosen by God to lead and save an entire nation; a nation that had turned away from the Lord and turned to idolatry. Gideon was called to lead a nation that had forgotten the God of their salvation, the God who now had the charge of leading 300 men into battle against a devastating 32,000.

Where would his strength come from? To whom could he look for aid, but God? To whom could he attribute a victory, although seemingly unlikely, but to the hand of the Lord? *"And the Angel of the Lord appeared to him, and said to him, "The Lord is with you, you mighty man of valor!" (Judges 6:12 NKJV)*

These words were spoken to Gideon directly, yet Gideon still buckled in disbelief. This was seen when Gideon proceeded to ask for not one, not two, but three separate signs of confirmation of his call.

It was in the impossibility of the ordeal that God demonstrated His glory. The angel of the Lord was able to beckon the cowering Gideon and address him as a "mighty man of valour." The angel of the Lord referred to Gideon as such, not because of what Gideon was doing, but for who he was becoming.

The enemy continually attempts to show us the unfinished product of who we are. Yet, God has a very contrary view on the subject; God wishes to show us the big picture. He does this so that we may no longer cower in a state of stagnation and fear; but instead, we will rise up and charge into the midst of the battle, knowing that in the end, we win.

We therefore may now analyze the blinding contrast between what the enemy tries to feed our minds with, and what God is speaking into our spirit. They are grossly contrary: The devil tells us that we are timid and cowardly; God in turn calls us mighty men and women of valour. The devil calls us weak and inadequate; God says, *"Beat your ploughshares into swords and your pruning hooks into spears. Let the weakling say, I am strong!" (Joel 3:10 NIV)*

The devil convinces us to detest living a holy life because he tells us that we are hopelessly unrighteous and unclean. God tells us through His word that we can be **"filled with the fruits of righteousness which are by Jesus Christ unto the glory and praise of God."** *(Philippians 1:11 NKJV)*

The enemy would have us to believe that we remain dead in trespasses and sin; therefore bound to repeatedly live defeated lives, working against the will of God and His precepts. God says, we were **"buried with Him** *(Christ)* **in baptism, in which you also were raised with Him through faith in the working of God, who raised Him from the dead."** (Colossians 2:12 NKJV)

Furthermore, the glorious thing is that it doesn't end there. Because Christ was raised from the dead, it is with that confidence that we can resolve to believe that "in him we live, and move, and have our being; as certain also of your own poets have said, for we are also his offspring." (Acts 17:28 NKJV)

It is therefore imperative to be able to see the big picture. Whose report will you believe?

Alone, Gideon could not have done it. Gideon stood with only 300 men, which was hardly enough to be relevant in battle, much less, expecting to be victorious against 32,000 men. Yet Gideon prevailed; but how?

> *"And he divided the three hundred men into three companies, and he put a trumpet in every man's hand, with empty pitchers, and lamps within the pitchers." (Judges 7:16 KJV)*

THE TRUMPET is symbolic of praise and a declaration of warfare. The Israelites were about to take the battle to the Midianites at full force. They were going in the name of the Lord, and in the strength and power of His might. It is in the atmosphere of praises that God inhabits. It was for this same reason that when the children of Israel later found themselves in conflict with the tribe of Benjamin at Gibeah, they inquired of the Lord as to who should go up FIRST into the battle at Gibeah, that the Lord replied, "JUDAH."

> *"The people of Israel arose and went up to Bethel and inquired of God, 'Who shall go up first for us to fight against the people of Benjamin?' And the LORD said, "Judah shall go up first." Then the people of Israel rose in the morning and encamped against Gibeah. [20] And the men of Israel went out to fight against Benjamin, and the men of Israel drew up the battle line against them at Gibeah. The people of Benjamin came out of Gibeah and destroyed on that day 22,000 men of the Israelites. (Judges 20:18-21 ESV)*

Here we have two separate instances of the Children of Israel being involved in a battle of seemingly insurmountable odds. In both situations they share a common factor: Praise. Of course there is no record of the children of Israel actually having a ceremony of praise prior to each battle; but if we look at each circumstance closely, we will see that in one battle the Children of Israel were instructed to blow *trumpets* before the battle began. The trumpet is an instrument of praise. The other incident occurred at the battle against Benjamin, where the children of Israel were instructed to send Judah first.

The word Judah means *praise*. In every battle the believer encounters, the first call of duty is to praise! Before you step into the boardroom and the corporate offices, the first call of duty is to praise! Before you step into the classroom or situate yourself at your place of work, your duty is to praise! *"Let everything that breathes sing praises to the LORD! Praise the LORD!" (Psalm 150:6 NLT).*

For God abides in the atmosphere of our praise and adoration. There is a copiousness of liberty in the presence of the Lord; for it is there in that atmosphere of praise, that His spirit sheds His glory amongst His people. So in the darkness of the night, sing praises unto God. He will shine a light even in the dark tunnels of total despair and utter confusion. He will speak to the wind and the billows in your life, and they will cease. The storm will pass after a while.

These struggles are only fanning the flames to a fire that will burn intensely and internally, and those flames will be used for the refining of your character. Although the enemy has evil intentions for our life experiences, God's plan is to allow every situation to work out for our betterment. **"You intended to harm me, but God intended it all for good. He brought me to this position so I could save the lives of many people."** *(Genesis 50:20 NLT)*

This was Joseph's testimony concerning the affliction that he endured, which was primarily caused by the jealousy of his brothers. They may have had bad intentions, but God allowed those fiery situations to prolong, in order to create something good. It is in the midst of this refiner's fire that you will discover new revelation of who you currently are, in contrast to who God has called you to be.

So with this knowledge, praise Him in difficult times; praise Him in times of sorrow. Praise Him when all hell breaks loose in your life. For even within those seasons of bewilderment, God will still show Himself to be strong. **"When they call on me, I will answer; I will be with them in trouble. I will rescue and honor them."** *(Psalm 91:15 NLT)*

THE EMPTY PITCHERS in *Judges 7:16* are symbolic of the believer's surrendered life. Pitchers were earthen vessels, which were mostly used to carry liquids. In the Word, believers are also described as "earthen vessels." The fact that the pitchers were empty implies that God's desire is that His people would become available, unreserved, and ready to be filled by Him.

> *"But we have this treasure in earthen vessels, that the excellence of the power may be of God and not of us." (2 Corinthians 4:7 NKJV)*

The treasure is God Himself. It is His anointing, the indwelling power of the Holy Ghost. We have this treasure inside our mortal bodies, which are but earthen vessels, temporal and imperfect. It is after God fills us with His Spirit that we become warriors for Christ, and we become equipped with all of our weapons of warfare; which *"are not carnal, but mighty through God to the pulling down of strong holds." (2 Corinthians 10:4 KJV)*

It is by the *breaking* of these earthen vessels that we grasp the understanding of what God intends to do with His people. He wants us to be broken of our own will, so that the will and purpose of God would pour out of us through His anointing.

"And it shall come to pass in that day, that his burden shall be taken away from off thy shoulder, and his yoke off thy neck, and the yoke shall be destroyed because of the anointing."
(Isaiah 10:27 KJV)

It is God's anointing that breaks the yoke. It is through the breaking of our vessels that we allow God to pour out what He has poured in. It is in the breaking of our vessels, our earthen vessels, that we release the awesome power of His anointing. It is during that time that God reigns in our lives. When we become surrendered to Him totally and completely, He pours out of us all that we need to fight and to endure the journey. But the vessel must be broken. Like Mary of Bethany, who approached Jesus and worshipped by outpouring that which was of great value, we too must break the box.

"While he was in Bethany, reclining at the table in the home of a man known as Simon the Leper, a woman came with an alabaster jar of very expensive perfume, made of pure nard. She broke the jar and poured the perfume on his head." (Mark 14:3 NIV)

No matter the protocol of religious restrictions that we may encounter, there comes a time when all protocol must cease. You might eventually reach a place where you are so bottled up inside that you want nothing else but God. The protocol becomes irrelevant, the camouflage becomes detectable; and all that's left to do is to...break the box! Your soul cries out for the living God to flow and become tangible in your life. The rituals and the ceremonial routines are no longer appealing. You just want to touch God. You just want to wash His feet with your tears. You just want to tell Him, *"While on others you are calling, DO NOT PASS ME BY! Saviour, Blessed Saviour, do not pass me by."*

As depicted in Judges 7:16, the Israelites were also given *LAMPS*, which were placed inside the pictures. The lamps are significant of the immutable word of God: ***"Thy word is a lamp unto my feet, and a light unto my path." (Psalm 119:105 KJV)***

> ***"Then the Lord turned to him and said, "Go with the strength you have, and rescue Israel from the Midianites. I am sending you!"" (Judges 6:14 NLT)***

Gideon and his troops were now walking with the word of God. He had promised to deliver the Israelites and His word cannot fail. It must come to pass, it is this Light, this Lamp, this Word that should keep us aflame and assured as we enter into the battlefields of life. God said He would, therefore, He must! He is faithful. God shines in the darkness of the impossible. He is present with us during moments of turmoil. Because this remains true, ***"we are troubled on every side, yet not distressed; we are perplexed but not in despair, persecuted but not forsaken, cast down, but not destroyed." (2 Corinthians 4:8-9 KJV)***

> ***"Then the three companies blew the trumpets and broke the pitchers—they held the torches in their left hands and the trumpets in their right hands for blowing—and they cried, "The sword of the Lord and of Gideon!" And every man stood in his place all around the camp; and the whole army ran and cried out and fled. When the three hundred blew the trumpets, the Lord set every man's sword against his companion throughout the whole camp; and the army fled to Beth Acacia, toward Zererah, as far as the border of Abel Meholah, by Tabbath." (Judges 7:20-22 NKJV)***

At the end of the day, God will prevail. He is ever faithful to His word. "*It is the same with my word. I send it out, and it always produces fruit. It will accomplish all I want it to, and it will prosper everywhere I send it.*" *(Isaiah 55:11 NLT)* The battle belongs to the Lord. When we allow him to fight through us, we win.

THE FIGHT

I've found myself on the battlefield of promise; fighting an enemy I can't physically see.

But I continue to fight through this dangerous plight; my weapons aren't carnal so I fight spiritually. I fight with all my might; sometimes I fight with a glimmer of fear. But this fear is soon dispelled, as my militant general draws near. He tells me to fight the enemy without remorse, take no prisoners, for the violent takes the kingdom by force. Forward still is Jehovah's will, though the enemy may rage and his kingdom may roar. I will continue to run forward and not be weary, on wings of victory I will soar.

So I will not retreat; I will not give in. The purpose within is in me to win. I know in whom I believe and I am persuaded to progress. I will not buckle beneath the burden of the test. I cannot fail, I will no longer stumble. I will not break; I refuse to crumble. Instead, I will prostrate upon my face, cry out to God and remain humble.

The God I serve has not forsaken me; he's already given me the victory. The battle ahead is no match for a King, for the battle is the Lord's. Songs of triumph I will sing. I've come too far, I've seen too much. I've heard His voice I've felt his touch, the gentle touch of his saving grace; I long to look upon his face. To see the face of him who died for me, the one who shed his blood on Calvary. "Such love, such wondrous love, that God should love a sinner such as I." (C. Bishop; Robert Harkness) Daily on his strength I've grown to rely. My sins have been forgiven; my life has been renewed. No longer bound by confusion; no longer misconstrued.

Now I see my destiny, now I believe my purpose. Now I empty myself of disbelief, now I give back to him my trust. *I now choose to trust Jesus with my whole heart; in so doing, I've relinquished my reliance on my own understanding.* From His presence I will no longer depart, even when the trial becomes rigid and demanding. For sometimes we're tempted to buckle beneath the pressure. Often we're tempted to be comforted by carnal pleasure. But a lifetime of purpose is far more valuable than a moment of sin. The enemy wants to cripple you; He wants to see you rescind. For a crippled soldier is of little use on the battlefield. During these times of testing we're often beguiled to yield.

But my friend, focus your eyes on glory; continue to spread the redemption story. Put up your dukes and press on in the fight, stray neither to the left nor to the right. But press forward still, even in the darkness of the night. Even when you grow weak and your faith grows dim, your spiritual light will He ignite.

So let us fight until day breaks, fight until a victor out of you he makes. Yet, we are already conquerors, even in the midst of the battle. So ride on towards sure vindication, do not shake do not be rattled, remain entrenched upon your saddle. Ride on, my soldier, ride on to victory; ride on, until you crush the head of the enemy.

> *"Blessed be the Lord my strength which teacheth my hands to war, and my fingers to fight." (Psalm 144:1 KJV)*

CHAPTER 12

THE PACIFIER

The devil's desire is to hold you in a state of spiritual infancy, until you become so comfortable in that state that you abort your purpose. Inactivity and stagnancy will cripple you and hold your purpose under siege. You will forever remain mediocre if you continue to operate in a stagnant routine. If you desire an extraordinary manifestation, you will have to initiate an extraordinary experience. If you are waiting on the manifestation of your purpose to simply fall into your hands, it isn't about to happen that way; it must be pursued. You have a responsibility concerning the gift that God has placed within you. It is for the edification and advancement of the Body of Christ.

If your gifting is not used so that you may be effective and affective in the Kingdom, you exist far beneath your Godly privilege, and also in a state of insignificance.

It isn't sufficient to simply be present on the battlefield in the Kingdom; it is necessary that you become an active, fierce warrior for Christ. March into the enemy's camp and take back every vision, every ounce of joy, every desire you had concerning your purpose. Take your anointing back, take your peace back, and tell the enemy that you are no longer travelling with the spirit of fear amongst your entourage. You now travel with power and a sound mind. Take back everything the enemy has stolen from you. It's yours and God wants you to have it, but you must take it by force.

The purpose and plan of God isn't a fairytale, as the devil would have you to believe. It isn't a theoretical ideology that is just repeated vainly and never manifested. We've already established that your purpose is the reason that you are here on earth; it is the reason for your existence in its totality. Therefore, it seems logical to state that each moment outside of your purpose might very well be a complete and utter waste of time.

The devil doesn't mind when we attend church services week after week, bring our largest Bible to Bible Study, with notepads in hand; or have our cars excessively covered with bumper stickers proclaiming: "Jesus saves." No, the devil doesn't really mind all that as much as we think he does. If he can get you to believe that such routine solely comprises the absolute capsule of Christianity, and that doing all of the above means that you've arrived at being a mature Christian, then he's got you exactly where he wants you. Going through routines and merely attending church services cannot be your destination as a believer. There is something more, something far more; and the excess can only be found when the revelation of your purpose occurs. But revelation concerning your calling must supersede the words spoken from a pulpit. Many of us are waiting on a fresh word to fall from heaven out of the mouth of a travelling evangelist. Although all of that is entirely possible, it is dangerous to bank all our hopes on receiving the typical confirmation of purpose. You know the kind I'm referring to; some preacher, prophet, or evangelist calls us from amongst the crowd and speaks life into us, and says, *"Brother Timmy, thus says the Lord, there is great destiny on your life, the Spirit of the Lord confirms it, go forth and preach the gospel!"* Oh yes, I think that's the type of confirmation that many of us are waiting on. But if you are, you might find yourself waiting for quite a long time, because God doesn't necessarily operate in that fashion at all times.

Regardless of who does or does not speak words of destiny over your life, true revelation must be confirmed within your own spirit. This revelation of purpose can only be attained through intimacy with God; and because God is a spirit, our flesh must die in order for us to truly connect with Him. You must free yourself from the shackles of carnal habits that the enemy has used to hold you captive. It is time now to relinquish those carnal addictions that the enemy uses to pacify you, while he hypnotizes you into a state of spiritual slumber.

Wake up soldier! Shake yourself from the dust. It is time to arise and conquer. Renew your covenant with God, grab hold of your weapons of warfare; trample on the head of the enemy and begin to walk in the Spirit. Choose life today and abandon the works of the flesh. It is time to arise, great soldier. The enemy knows who you are; do you?

Now, I encourage you to dig deep within that treasure chest that is inside of you, and pull out from within the many gifts that have been locked and stored away. *"Therefore I remind you to stir up the gift of God which is in you through the laying on of my hands." (2 Timothy 1:6 NKJV)*

Many have interpreted this scripture to mean that the revelation of our gift and purpose can only be affirmed or revealed in a ceremonial tradition that involves a third-party. Such a perspective of this scripture would be flawed, for a few reasons; but primarily because it would place the limitation of your purpose literally in the hands of another individual. This of course was not the intention of this scripture, and receiving it as such would take the text out of context. This particular text is a part of a letter from Paul, which was specifically written to Timothy, bringing to remembrance the circumstances that surrounded Timothy's ascension into ministry. The apostle Paul recognized the need to encourage the young leader to continue in the path that he began, and to help Timothy to realize the great capacity of his potential. The text was not intended to be a blue-print routine of how we are to receive the revelation of our purpose. I admonish you to stop waiting on external forces to confirm what God has already spoken into your spirit. No political or social agenda will propel you into the realm of your ministry. Your purpose is not predicated on the opinion or the influence of man. You must understand and truly believe that promotion comes from no other source but the Lord.

> *"No one from the east or the west or from the desert can exalt themselves. It is God who judges: He brings one down, he exalts another. In the hand of the LORD is a cup full of foaming wine mixed with spices; he pours it out, and all the wicked of the earth drink it down to its very dregs. As for me, I will declare this forever; I will sing praise to the God of Jacob, who says, "I will cut off the horns of all the wicked, but the horns of the righteous will be lifted up." (Psalm 75:6-10 NIV)*

If you find yourself tired of being mediocre, tired of consistently retreating again and again, only to have to go through the frustrating reality of fighting the same battles while trying to conquer the same demons that have been attacking your mind, ministry, finances and family, then you're probably ready to exit the womb of purpose. The water is about to break and a birthing of your purpose is now imminent, and you will begin to exist in a new dimension. In this dimension, we will no longer take advantage of God's grace as we did before. We now recognize that God desires to elevate us from a posture of continuously walking as spirited junkies. This condition is when one falls in love with the concept of godliness, but doesn't really desire a genuine relationship with God. So like a junky, he finds God during the seasons when he needs a quick fix.

If you're familiar with the behaviour of one who is habituated to any form of substance abuse, you can identify that it isn't important for this addict to even have a relationship with the individual that supplies what he needs. In fact, he doesn't even really need to know his name. All that this addict needs to know is that when he wants that quick fix, he can get it from…that guy, from Building Ten on the corner of 5th street. He knows where to go to meet this nameless friend, and he knows all the protocol of being discreet. He even knows the secret language that they both use during their many transactions. You know, the street language; now a measure of cocaine is no longer called Cocaine, it becomes "C-dust," or "C-game," or even some "California Cornflakes." PCP is no longer PCP; no, in the language of the streets it's referred to as "Cliff-hanger," "Crazy Eddie," or the more popular name, "Angel Dust." A bag of marijuana is no longer called Marijuana, but instead, the addict walks up to his dealer and asks for some "Laughing Grass," "Catnip," "Chicago Green," or quite simply, some "Trees."

Oh yeah, the addict is familiar with the language, but he still doesn't really know the person that's supplying his need; after all, he doesn't need to. Why bother become acquainted, when the extent of the relationship is only for those few moments when the dealer enables him to get high? Why would he become friendly when the addict simply wants to leave the troubles of this world for a moment and just feel good, just for a little while? The dealer would never call this addict a friend, but they have a common language, and that's good enough for the addict. All he needs is a quick fix; the addict has no time for a friendship or small talk.

In this conversation, you'll never hear the questions, "So, how are the wife and kids? How's the new job coming along?" Nope, the addict is there for nothing but the fix. So for the entire duration of the addiction, that dealer, the guy from building ten on the corner of 5th street, remains a stranger.

Sadly, some Christians can be likened to this addict in regards to their relationship with Christ. They've become *spirited junkies* who have a fashion of godliness, but they ignore the power that God possesses, because they choose to remain in a sinful state; periodically running in and out of the presence of God, while trying to satisfy their conscience. They do this while thinking, *"As long as every now and then I'm quickened by the Spirit, as long as in the presence of worship I speak more words in unknown tongues than I do in English, I'm doing alright."*

Such is the life of a spirited junky; not spiritual, but a *spirited* junky. So this junky gets delivered and repents. He becomes temporarily grateful to God for delivering him from the sinful state, so he worships and rejoices. This worship isn't necessarily insincere; in his heart he may sincerely have a desire to please God; but that desire is diluted by the crippling power of his addiction, sin. As a result, very shortly after, this spirited junky returns to the same repugnant situation in which he previously dwelled. The charismatic experience has become his high. For this junky, The Holy Spirit, for all intensive purpose has been carved into the role of the dealer. But this addict is only masking the core of his condition with momentary thrills of religious activity. He isn't close enough to this dealer to actually experience any measure of intimacy, neither does he share the fact that he is deeply wounded and hurting and he's actually in need of much more than a shout.

> **"On that day many will say to me, 'Lord, Lord, did we not prophesy in your name, and cast out demons in your name, and do many mighty works in your name?' And then will I declare to them, 'I never knew you; depart from me, you workers of lawlessness.'" (Matthew 7:22-23 ESV)**

However, if you've found yourself being able to relate to the addict, I declare that there is hope for you; but you must submit to a state of true repentance. True repentance encompasses a change of heart. If you can identify with any of the above behaviour, I encourage you to break away from the addiction of being pacified into a state of mediocrity and stagnation. Your purpose cannot be manifested until it is first acknowledged, received and passionately pursued.

Irrespective of how large or even how insignificant you may think that your calling is, ignore that notion, go ahead and grab a hold of faith and begin to pursue your purpose. Whatever it is that God has assigned to your earthly vessel, receive it boldly and run after it diligently.

I CRIED

I sat one night contemplating my spiritual fight,
contemplating the dimming of my spiritual light.
I had lost focus, strayed away from my purpose.
My trials consumed my faith like a locust.
And so I became blinded by my plight;
Let me tell you, I wasn't living too right.
And so in remorse, I cried to my maker, the Father of Lights.

My judgment was clouded and my life was a mess
Couldn't figure out why I traded my faith for this stress.
The temporary pleasures I indulged in, couldn't
compensate for the pain I felt within.
No compensation, no paycheque, no woman, no material
thing could ever take the place of the purpose within.
Yet, still, I strayed and walked in a life of sin.

But in the darkness of the nights I cried, for
internally there was a divine unrest.
For even in the midst of my test,
the Lord still spoke to me and declared that for me, he wanted the best:

"Where are you my child, have you forgotten me?
Why do you run from your awesome destiny?
The trials you endure are for your good.
So stand now as the man of valour, as you know you should."

So many nights He spoke these words into my spirit, but still
confused, I continued to run away. My redemption was nigh but I just
couldn't see it; so while I cried, I continued to stray. Each night I cried,
and I cried again; knowing that I had forsaken my spiritual friend.

But one morning bright and early I bended my knees and prayed that
the Lord would deliver me. I wanted to restore my purpose and destiny.
And so I cried aloud with cloven tongues of fire,
beseeching God to remove all of my carnal desire.

From sin and shame I now wanted to retire.

Then the words from His throne came back to me,
In a still calm voice He spoke peaceably:

"My child, as far as the east is from the west
So I've removed from you your sin and all your mess.
I've taken away all your carnal habits. I've
taken away all your addictions.
I've reignited your spiritual convictions; no
longer exist in the cycle of repetition:
In which I washed you and redeemed your soul;
Cleansed and made you whole.
Then you returned back to the vomit of your sin,
back to the carnal habits to once again begin.
No, no more of that my son, today you are a victor.
I've removed the cloud from your eyes so that
you may see my divine picture.
You may now see the plan I've ordained for your life;
Now you can see who I've designed you to be.
I've removed from you the burden and the strife;
I've given you clear vision of your destiny."

And so after I received these words of promise and hope from my
maker, I began to cry. For on my own strength I no longer had to rely.
But this time when I cried they were tears of joy and victory.
As I began now to contemplate on the grace that was given to me.
I was excited about the new journeys I would make.
But this time around, it was the road of purpose that I wanted to take.
No more retreating no more inconsistency,
no more sequels of my mistakes.
I've now learnt how to stand.
I've now learnt what it really means to be a man.

But do real men cry? Some may say.
To you who ask, I offer these two words today: "Jesus wept."

…Oh yes he did!
Jesus wept, and a greater man has never lived.
And he indeed was even greater than just a man.
He is and was the Incarnate Word; the Bread of
Life, in Him is embedded the redemption plan. For
the first man failed and fell from grace,
And so in shame Adam hid himself from God's face

So many today are doing the same; running away because of shame.
The shame of sin has marred your focus.
But I say to you, return to the potter's wheel;
All your hurt and wounds he longs to heal.
He will restore to you his joy and peace, if
only to Jesus …you would cry.

CHAPTER 13

<u>VIRTUAL REALITY</u>

During the early 1990's the video game world was swarmed with a vast increase of computerized games. During this era, gamers were introduced to a plethora of new digitized games that presented to the player an experience of life-like applications, all controlled by a device held in the palm of the hand. This concept took off like wildfire. Soon, every video game system had a variety of games that made the player feel like they were actually inside the television, living the events that were transpiring before their eyes.

The games varied from bloody, high-flying, hard kicking, martial arts games, to simply driving in an Indy 500 vehicle, while racing around a track at exorbitant speeds. Imagine doing all of that without ever actually having to leave your couch. It was a great new experience for those who wanted to feel the excitement that came with such events, but simultaneously didn't want to risk the danger of actually doing any of the above in real life.

So the world of virtual reality grew and grew. It even expanded into the realm of the erotic. All of a sudden, everything was a virtual game, even sex. So the introduction of Cyber-Sex was also on the rise. It was no longer enough to simply view pornographic material; now, technology introduced a method that revolutionized the concept of sex.

So being virtually real almost became more appealing than reality itself. As for those individuals who couldn't or wouldn't engage in the reality of life, virtual reality was not only a safe haven, it also brought to their doors what they couldn't otherwise achieve or experience.

Now, quite a few years have passed by since the introduction of virtual reality games and activities. Today, reality TV dictates to us that people want to now experience life, with all the danger and excitement that comes along with it. We have TV shows that leave individuals stranded on deserted islands, simply to observe the nature of their behaviour and their survival techniques.

Others base an entire show on the social activity of a group of young people gathered together at an exotic location, engaging in promiscuous behaviour and generally just making fools out of themselves on national television. Yet, each season, the ratings go off the charts; apparently, that is exactly what the world wants to see.

Sadly, some Christians also fall in the above categories as spectators to these programs that make zombies out of them, while they live their lives through other people. But the fact is, in essence, these actions still equate to a form of virtual reality; because one person lives the life, and the other takes the delight in watching them live it.

As much as we may refuse to accept it, many Christians are still stuck in a state of virtual reality; except, here is the problem: Our state of virtual reality transcends any form of technological entertainment. We've become "virtual" concerning our purpose and calling. We go to convention after convention, after convention, and listen to speaker after speaker after speaker; yet, after the shout is over, we've accomplished nothing, we do nothing, and we produce nothing.

We allow the message to become more exciting than the method. But I believe that it isn't enough to talk about the Promised

Land, if when we finally get there, no one wants to enter the land for fear of the conflicts that they have to endure.

> *"They gave Moses this account: 'we went into the land to which you sent us, and it does flow with milk and honey! Here is its fruit. But the people who live there are powerful, and the cities are fortified and very large…'" (Numbers 13:27-28 NIV)*

If something isn't worth fighting for, then it isn't worth having. If the value of possessing it doesn't outweigh the risk of claiming it, then there is no point in pursuing it. If we know that our prize is as valuable as we believe it to be, we cannot allow the fear of conflict to cripple us, and cause us to become immobile in the pursuit of our purpose and destiny.

It is during these times that it is important to be surrounded by great individuals who are doers. In the face of the opposition, all the theories and strategies become ineffective unless they are actually put to practice. Fear says, "what if?" Faith says, "Let's do it!"

Of course there is nothing wrong in considering our options and being cautious in our progress. But it is fear that materializes when God has given us specific instruction and we are still asking Him, "What if?"

> *"Then Caleb silenced the people before Moses and said, we should go up and take possession of the land, for we can certainly do it." (Numbers 13:30 NIV)*

Great leaders do not buckle under the pressure of opposition. Great leaders recognize that the victory lies in the fight, not just in the triumph. In other words, there is no glory in achieving a prize if you know that you've never participated in the race.

CHAPTER 14

<u>CREAM OF THE CROP</u>

For the first eleven years of my life I lived in what I believe to be one of the most beautiful islands in the Caribbean, the island of Jamaica. From a young age, I was drawn to a variety of sporting activities. The first of these was Track & Field. Now, it was a custom for us to compete in what was then called "house leagues." In the house leagues, we competed against our peers who were all students in the same school. During that time, there were many children that got to participate. These track meets served as a qualifying process to determine the greatest and fastest athletes. Once that was determined, these top athletes were then considered as the cream of the crop, and they were therefore chosen to represent their school in the Primary School Championship that eventually included young athletes from across the nation.

To make a long story quite short, at that time, there was very little cream in my crop. It took me a while to realize that it wasn't so much that I was so terrible, but instead, they were simply that great. I did eventually propel that passion towards other avenues in which I was more equipped, and therefore finding my niche in the area of athletics.

However, my memories of that particular championship were spent in the stands cheering, as the representative ran on behalf of our school. As the saying goes, I was not a very happy camper.

As adults, we can appreciate the notion of being a "team player," and we can grasp the concept of *"when one team member wins, we all win."* Sure, right now, all of that sounds dandy, and beaming with the essence of sportsmanship. But to a 9-year-old boy who stood pouting because I wasn't the one being cheered for, sportsmanship wasn't easily embraced. All I wanted was to be the one on those blocks, as the starter raised his hands in the air and fired the starter pistol. I could imagine flying through the lanes like Carl Lewis himself, changing batons and being ahead of the pack. Okay ...ok, I'll admit it: I was a sore loser! But that being said, the disappointment that I so childishly exhibited, along with the negative motive of pride, instilled in me an eternal fight that craved the glory of the victory. I thirsted for the heat of the competition. Competition, when fuelled by the right spirit, can sometimes be a very constructive tool for motivating purpose.

Although this juvenile analogy is more comical than it is practical, it was drawn to paint the picture that victory is sometimes also simply enduring the challenge itself. Victory sometimes means being able to stand against opposition and being able to say, *"I did it; I stepped up to the plate, I didn't back down and I made it through to the very bitter end."* Sometimes that in itself is a victory. Sometimes victory is showing up to the battle, being present and no matter how hard it gets, not giving up until the battle is over. I desired to at least be given the opportunity to confront that challenge. But such opportunities aren't *given*, they must be earned.

> *"So Jacob was left alone, and a man wrestled with him till daybreak. When the man saw that he could not overpower him, he touched the socket of Jacob's hip so that his hip was wrenched as he wrestled with the man. Then the man said, 'Let me go, for it is daybreak.' But Jacob replied, 'I will not let you go unless you bless me.' The*

*man asked him, 'What is your name?' 'Jacob,'
he answered. Then the man said, 'Your name
will no longer be Jacob, but Israel, because you
have struggled with God and with men and have
overcome.'" (Genesis 32:24-28 NIV)*

Being a spectator all our lives offers no true reward. Because at the end of that journey, all we would be able to say was that "yeah, I was there." Being a spectator usually means that someone, either ourselves or others, have predetermined that we do not even qualify to participate in this event. Many times, in the journey of life, we are the ones who often make that self-disqualifying assessment.

On the contrary, I believe that my heavenly Father has already predetermined that I'm not only fit to participate, I am already deemed to be a winner! It is therefore our own perceptions that get in the way, and impedes us from rising up and being conquerors on the battlefields of life. It is the image of defeat, which we choose to paint, that creates a distraction for us as we fight life's battles. That false view of ourselves subsequently smears our focus.

In contrast to the story of my poor Track and Field performance, I'm reminded of an athlete whose greatness is undeniable; he has been the epitome of excellence on the track. I think it is safe to say that we probably might never see another individual who mirrors his athletic ability, while demonstrating such charisma. That athlete is of course, Usain Bolt. His display of talent in his legendary athletic career has been unparalleled. He has achieved so much success and has become a philanthropist within his own nation. All these things are absolutely factual, and his success is definitely a reality. However, Usain Bolt didn't just wake up one day and become successful. There was a process; there was a journey. Every process has a beginning.

This was Usain Bolt's beginning: Of course, like most track athletes, Bolt began competing as a child while in school; even during those early years of youth, Usain had already accomplished much success. His first Olympic competition in the 200m race occurred at the Athens Olympics in 2004. However, the result of that showing was not quite favorable. The 17-year-old Bolt had already won many races prior to this point, and he had become a star on the national level in Jamaica; but on this particular day in Athens, there were at least FOUR other men who were more spectacular at their craft than he was.

That was then, and this is now. Now, none of those four men who beat the young Bolt can be found in any place of dominance in Track and Field history, and yet Bolt now stands as a Legend. The moral of the story is: Don't fall in love with the glamour without understanding the process. Bolt's success is no accident; it takes continuous hard work, perseverance, and determination. So does your journey.

Bolt did not do well on his Olympic debut, and you too may be experiencing some life altering struggle. But your latter will be greater than your past. If you endure the process, someday you could be great. If you endure the pain, someday you will win. If you don't quit, your past defeat of yesterday will only make you a stronger champion tomorrow. Endure the process. There is greatness within you.

Turmoil and defeat will often bury the seed of your purpose, but if you keep on cultivating, your determination will water the root of purpose and the brilliance of your perseverance will cause excellence to spring forth. Don't give up on the seed; it has to die in order for the fruit to live. Cherish every minute of your growth, even the moments of defeat. Endure the process.

Your view of yourself will determine the direction of your journey. Your opinion of yourself is so much more important than what others think of you. This isn't from an egotistical focus, but rather from the awareness that people's opinion will sway with inconsistency like the wind. Therefore, do not allow the opinion of others to be the sculpture of your identity.

> *"Then the men who had gone up with him said, "We are not able to go up against the people, for they are stronger than we are." So they brought to the people of Israel a bad report of the land that they had spied out, saying, "The land, through which we have gone to spy it out, is a land that devours its inhabitants, and all the people that we saw in it are of great height. And there we saw the Nephilim (the sons of Anak, who come from the Nephilim), and we seemed to ourselves like grasshoppers, and so we seemed to them." (Numbers 13:31-33 ESV)*

Whatever you think of yourself that is what you will become. Whatever the identity you project to others, generally, that is how you will be perceived. You hold the keys of your identity; don't give anyone access to the corridors of your mind, so that they can walk right in and plant seeds of negativity within you. Guard your mind against negative notions that hold no other purpose except to cut you down. Resist the infiltration of negative thoughts that threaten to dethrone your security. Insecurity is a violent weed, and if it is allowed to grow, it will strangle the cultivation of your purpose.

Dispel every defeatist attitude from your mind, and rest in the security of the Lord.

"Don't worry about anything; instead, pray about everything. Tell God what you need, and thank him for all he has done. Then you will experience God's peace, which exceeds anything we can understand. His peace will guard your hearts and minds as you live in Christ Jesus. And now, dear brothers and sisters, one final thing. Fix your thoughts on what is true, and honorable, and right, and pure, and lovely, and admirable. Think about things that are excellent and worthy of praise. Keep putting into practice all you learned and received from me—everything you heard from me and saw me doing. Then the God of peace will be with you." (Philippians 4:6-9 NLT)

<u>SHADOW</u>

There is a shadow, a shadow following me, a shadow portraying the man I used to be, a shadow taunting me, haunting me, telling me who I cannot be. He tells me I cannot be because of who I used to be, cannot be because of the past that I have that others do not see. Cannot be because of the existence of insecurity, and because of the reputation of impurity, he says I cannot be the man God has ordained in me. At times this shadow even proceeds before me, preventing me from seeing my destiny. But when I see the reality of the shadow chasing me, I see that it is being projected internally.

For we are told in biblical records that a few men went to investigate the Promised Land. Some came back with a good report and others came back with a fearful reprimand.

The latter of the two groups brought back their report and instead of giving a positive exhort, they came back to Moses and said: *"Great leader, listen, we'll make this short. In summary, these are the words of our report. We took a look at this so called Promised Land, and let me tell you, the men we saw had fingers the size of my hand. Yes, indeed there were giants in the land. We therefore now need to rethink our plan, because our previous strategy will not be able to stand. In our own eyes we are to them like grasshoppers, in our own eyes we are therefore vision stoppers, and therefore we can never rise above our enemy; because there is a shadow following me."*

But Caleb in his wisdom spoke to the cowering men and said: *"Listen men, we will not give in, I truly believe that we are well able to win, because though they are larger, fellows, we are stronger; it is the presence of God that makes us greater.*

God told us that he has already given to us the land; so what more is there to understand? Let us rise up now, don't ask me how; I just know that in this fight we will rise and conquer!"

> *"...Caleb quieted the people before Moses and said, "Let us go up at once and occupy it, for we are well able to overcome it." (Numbers 13:30 ESV)*

"Even though I walk through the valley of the shadow of death, I will fear no evil, for you are with me; your rod and your staff, they comfort me." (Psalm 23:4 ESV) So I am no longer fearful of the shadow that is following me. I find strength from the light that now burns internally, it burns ever so fervently, it burns with the passion of hope; having clear vision of purpose and destiny. So this is why I can passionately pursue my purpose. I recognize now the land that God had already given to us. I recognize it from afar, but though the journey is rather long, I will press on against the giants of the land; I boldly declare war.

I can no longer see the shadow following me. I now see the brightness of the Morning Star, leading me into the Promised Land. I decree that I will manifest God's divine plan. I will walk into the Promised Land, with no shadow, no negative report; just the garment of praise and the word of God in my hand. Those are all the weapons that I need; so that against the wiles of the enemy we will be able to succeed.

So my friend, if in your life you begin to see a shadow, a shadow that tells you that on the road of purpose you should no longer follow, a shadow that tells you that there is no hope in your tomorrow, remember the brave words of Joshua and Caleb: *"The land we traveled through and explored is a wonderful land! And if the LORD is pleased with us, he will bring us safely into that land and give it to us. It is a rich land flowing with milk and honey. Do not rebel against the LORD, and don't be afraid of the people of the land. They are only helpless prey to us! They have no protection, but the LORD is with us! Don't be afraid of them!" (Numbers 14:7-9 NLT)*

Listen my friend, don't you give in; you are more than able to win. You will indeed rise and conquer!

CHAPTER 15

<u>BE YOU</u>

When I was a teenager, during those blissful years when I was certain I knew everything, one day my mother said something to me that stuck with me ever since. She said, *"The man who you are going to be, you are now becoming."* At that time, I think I might have been just as puzzled as perhaps you are right now, as you're probably trying to figure out exactly what she meant by that. But then she explained further, and I got to understand what she was really saying. Everyone has a particular image of themselves in their mind as to who they are. When we were children, we were always pondering on who we would be; we had the understanding that we hadn't yet reached that final stage in our development, and we knew that we still had quite a distance to go in the journey of maturity. In knowing that, we began to devise an image in our mind of who we would be when we grew up. Many of us painted very influential personalities of prominence in our mind. We were taught that we should aspire to be lawyers, doctors, dentists and engineers, which are all wonderful *professions;* but none of those things qualify as *character traits.* Those are simply jobs, things that people do to acquire income.

But we are not what we do; we are instead the person that is presented from the contents of our character. We have been taught for so long to aspire to become these great professionals, to aspire to do these great things, and that we should have these great goals of achievement. Rightly so, but of course who we are has more to do with our character than our professional status.

My mother wasn't at all referring to my profession; she was indeed speaking about my character. What my mother was trying to tell me was simply this, I wasn't going to just wake up one day in the stage of my manhood and say, *"ok, that's it, I'm a good man now,"* or *"today I've decided that I will now begin to have integrity and good morals, and I will live in honesty and self-respect from this day forward."* No, it doesn't exactly work like that; character is a process of growth.

The statement my mother made was a simple one, but it had such a profound meaning to me. I eventually understood that she meant that I had to decide what type of man I wanted to be, even at that early stage of maturity. In that decision, my attitude, my behaviour and my focus would have to change in order to eventually fit into the mould of character that I wanted to emulate

I must therefore understand that in the process of pursuing purpose, the person I am becoming requires significantly more of my focus than the man I aspire to be. So indeed, my mother was right after all: *The man who I am going to be is the man I am becoming.* If I desire to achieve great things, I must be disciplined in the faithfulness of miniscule responsibility. I must learn consistency in small things and I must understand that every action in my life is a reflection of my current mentality, and my mentality determines the core of my character.

With that being said, I can only have peace of mind if I am becoming who I am suppose to be; rather than embracing the identity that is projected upon me, or adopting the image of someone else who I admire. When you cease from coveting the pathway of others, you will discover the excellence that is embedded within you. Why go through life living as a replica when your internal treasure is priceless and unique?

Therefore, don't go through life pretending to have a grasp on success while failing to be yourself. Any successful forgery is merely a failure at authenticity. Be yourself and pursue the excellence within. Shun the temptation of comparison; be you.

CHAPTER 16

<u>HARVEST TIME</u>

Who do you see yourself as? Your vision of who you are will most likely determine what others see in you. This is why it is important to surround yourself with individuals who are consistently speaking life into the core of your being, rather than polluting you with negative concepts that act as weeds in the garden of your purpose.

During the time of cultivation, the farmer's duty is to keep a careful watch of the weeds among the crop, which will inevitably grow among the desired fruit of any plantation. The farmer understands that the real threat isn't necessarily the fact that the weeds exist amongst the crop, the real threat occurs when those weeds begin to somehow stifle the crop; whether by crowding its territory or by excreting substances in the soil that are contrary to healthy cultivation.

Sometimes the plants that are potentially harmful to the crop do not resemble the expected appearance of weeds. Instead, these plants can appear just as indigenous to the plantation as the crop does; one such plant is the Sunflower plant.

The Sunflower plant has many uses and it isn't necessarily labelled as a weed. In fact, some may describe it as a beautiful flower in the garden; one that can grow up to eight, even twelve feet high, if cultivated in good soil. The fruits of this plant, which are merely seeds, are used both for bird feeding as well as human consumption. The seeds, when properly prepared, make for a convenient snack. However, the fact remains that despite all of these good uses, the sunflower plant is indeed an allelopathic plant. Such types of plants, although they present an image of beauty and even produce fruit, their presence may prove to be detrimental to other types of plants being cultivated amongst the same soil. This is because allelopathic plants such as sunflowers excrete a natural substance that is actually a chemical toxin. Such toxins attack the healthy development of other plants of different classifications that happen to share the same feeding ground.

Among other weeds, the sunflower is the farmer's best friend. On the contrary, among a garden of vegetables or other types of fruit yielding plants, the sunflower may not be such a desirable flower in that ecosystem. This is because the sunflower will operate in the same manner as it does with the smaller weeds. Therefore, it will hinder the produce of that plant and may eventually cause death resulting from its natural process of releasing these chemical toxins. This is relevant to the believer's life, because the Lord, who is our husbandman, our counsellor, and our farmer, is also concerned about the types of organisms that surround His crop. He therefore keeps a watchful eye on each stage of development of our purpose, in order to decipher which individuals are for our betterment and which are not.

"Children, time is just about up. You heard that Antichrist is coming. Well, they're all over the place, antichrists everywhere you look. That's how we know that we're close to the end. They left us, but they were never really with us. If they had been, they would have stuck it out with us, loyal to the end. In leaving, they showed their true colors, showed they never did belong."
(1 John 2:18-19 MSG)

The Farmer understands that there are some weeds that cause great damage to the crop, and others that may be a nuisance during cultivation. However, there are also other weeds that may cause no real threat to the produce of the crop. These weeds sometimes grow so intricately knit with the roots of the crop that the farmer may allow the weeds to grow alongside the crop until the time of harvest. It is during that time only, that the two are separated. *(Matthew 13:24:30 MSG) "He told another story. "God's kingdom is like a farmer who planted good seed in his field. That night, while his hired men were asleep, his enemy sowed thistles all through the wheat and slipped away before dawn. When the first green shoots appeared and the grain began to form, the thistles showed up, too. The farmhands came to the farmer and said, 'Master, that was clean seed you planted, wasn't it? Where did these thistles come from?' He answered, 'Some enemy did this.' The farmhands asked, 'Should we weed out the thistles?' He said, 'No, if you weed the thistles, you'll pull up the wheat, too. Let them grow together until harvest time. Then I'll instruct the harvesters to pull up the thistles and tie them in bundles for the fire, then gather the wheat and put it in the barn.'"*

During preparation for the harvest, we must not only know who our neighbours are in this garden of development, we must also be very cognizant of who we are in relation to our environment. Some environments are not conducive to our growth, and therefore, we must be plucked out of such environments and carefully engrafted into another. For certain type of plants, the new environment that they need to exist in is an environment of solitude.

Similar to the scenario of plants, people should also ensure that we exist within appropriate environments according to our individual needs. The stage of our development may dictate that we remain in a season of solitude in order to appropriately mature to the state that God requires of us.

In the wisdom of our Father, He is able to judge which circumstances demand that we become uprooted from our environment; as oppose to the other situations whereby the toxins are removed from amongst us. He is able to do it; He will, if needed.

Another method of disrupting the growth of weeds in a field of cultivation is by planting smother crop amongst them. Smother crop planting is a method of cultivation which strategically inserts special types of plants among a particular crop. The process involves plants that have a natural invasiveness about them. They grow in a way that they crowd the area in which they are planted.

Smother plants are usually planted in a bunch and purposely cluttered together. This method assures that the weeds around them will have no room to develop and therefore die out, right in the midst of the desired crop. This sounds like yet another demonstration of survival of the fittest.

It's for this reason that we shouldn't worry when individuals who are threatened by the growth of our purpose surround us. Leave them to the husbandman, the farmer, our Lord; He will decipher what needs to be done.

Sometimes, it is as simple as growing healthier, stronger and faster than those weeds around us. Therefore, ensuring that we aren't stifled by them; instead, we rise above their asphyxiating nature and prove to be the fittest in the crop.

In the pursuit of your purpose, your environment is crucial. An ideal atmosphere for healthy growth exists where you are able to develop your purpose amongst people who are going in the same direction as you. When you are battling in the boxing ring of life, you need people in your corner who are fighting for you rather than against you. These people in your corner should be resilient and determined individuals; you can't have quitters in your corner. There will be moments when you'll feel like quitting; you need a winner speaking into your ears in those moments. You need a fighter beside you who will not allow you to throw in the towel and abort your purpose. Choose your friends wisely.

The company that you keep should be a squad of champions. When you all unite and get connected, and sharpen each other with your gifting, you will also grow together and yield fruit during the time of harvest. A tight-knit alliance with diligent people is imperative. Your purposeful unity will not only help to stabilize your growth, it will simultaneously cause the trampling of the enemy, just by simply continuing to live victoriously.

> *"As iron sharpens iron, so a man sharpens the countenance of his friend." (Proverbs 27:17 NKJV)*

So when you are surrounded by weeds in your environment: at work, at school, in the various relationships of life, and yes, even in the church, just get close to those individuals who share a common goal. Stay connected to those who are passionately pursuing their purpose. Remain with them during your time of development and simply continue to live. Eventually, the passion that is attached to your gifting will drive away the weeds in your life, and make room enough for you to continue to grow in the field that God has established for you.

> *"A man's gift makes room for him, and brings him before great men." (Proverbs 18:16 NKJV)*

The cultivating stage is an interesting one. Even after reviewing all that we have concerning the behaviour of plants and their natural environment, the fact remains that as humans, we will need somebody at sometime in our lives. But we should be careful so that we are able to discern who we allow into our lives, so that our purpose doesn't become stifled by acts of stagnation. We can therefore continue to pursue our purpose with an intense desire.

"Those too lazy to plow in the right season will have no food at the harvest." (Proverbs 20:4 NLT)

It is now time to allow God to germinate that which He has established, and bring to maturation the seed that He has planted within you.

CHAPTER 17

<u>THE FIXER</u>

If you haven't met them as yet, you will meet someone like this at some point in your life that will appear to have all the answers to address each situation that you may encounter. Yet, beneath the surface, if you dig deep enough, you will discover that their life is a mess. These types of people are clumped under the category of The Fixer. Their life unfolds like the scenes of a badly written soap opera, yet they have become the self-appointed advisors of your life. They insist that no matter what the circumstance may be, they have a remedy that can fix you.

The Fixer: The individual who always wants to know how you are doing, but is secretly disappointed when your response is optimistic. The individual who has much to say about what is needed to correct your life, but who simultaneously has a perpetual storm occurring in their own.

No, I'm not referring to Olivia Pope, and no, this isn't a chapter about the next Scandal episode. The Fixer of whom I'm referring usually comes with a lot less celebrity status. You don't have to wait until 10pm Eastern Standard Time (EST) every Thursday night to meet this fixer, they are always around.

Throughout the journey of life there will always be some individuals who are addicted to human projects. Meaning, they have an almost unquenchable need to be the fixer of all broken things pertaining to other people. Now, had that been the entire picture, there would be nothing necessarily wrong with that. After all, who wouldn't receive with open arms a mender of broken things? Well, the dysfunctional reality occurs when these people are often broken themselves, and are simply afraid of diving into the deep dark crevices of their own life. That translates into them being more comfortable with your problems than they are with your progress.

They don't celebrate your accomplishments because it reminds them of their lack of success. They don't encourage your advancement because your stagnation pacifies their procrastination. They don't glory in your personal triumph, because they are more impressed by their own ability to provide a good pep-talk during the moments when you are down in the gutter. The drug of impartation is a distracting addiction that keeps their mind off of the mess that exists within them. They exist as supervising janitors in the lives of many, yet they have never before cleaned their own toilet. They have become experts of instructional remedies that have never actually been applied to their own life.

They reside in their storm because they are too lazy to endure the exodus. When your sad song becomes music to their ears, then you know you are dealing with a fixer. When your independent celebration brings a look of apathy on their face, you know you are dealing with a fixer. When they would rather see you down and out, rather than up and about and exhibiting victorious shouts, you know you have a fixer in your midst.

So, how do you get rid of them? That's an excellent question, I'm glad you asked.

The first step in dispelling the fixer once and for all: No matter how down you are feeling, no matter how rough a day, no matter how tumultuous your situation may be, never run to the fixer to gain shelter during your stormy season. He will not cover you. Running to a fixer when you have overwhelming circumstances feeds their consuming flame, and it is as efficacious as using kerosene oil to put out a grease fire.

Not everyone who bends an ear at your trial should be granted access to the intimate details of your life. Some people should simply be told to mind their own business, plain and simple. If it makes you feel better, you may say it like this, "Mind your own business, please; blessings." Try that.

The next step in getting rid of a fixer is to ensure that you do not become dependent on their bootleg advice. What's bootleg advice? Once again, that's an excellent question, I appreciate you asking that:

Anyone who obtains bootleg products possesses something or has access to something that he technically holds no legal claim on; because he has never spent the real value of what it is actually worth to acquire it. Bootleg advice is no different. If these people in your life are trying to sell you counsel for situations that they have never been in, and are giving you instructions to apply remedies that have not been proven in their own life, then that advice is, bootleg. We all know what happens to bootleg products, they don't last very long, and neither does such advice.

Seek individuals who aspire to propel you on an even higher plane than they currently reside. Walk with individuals who leap for joy when you succeed, and who are relieved when you find happiness. Keep the company of those who mourn in your sadness, celebrate in your gladness and protect the privacy of your failures with sincere confidentiality. Love covers.

The Fixer is not your friend. They have a convincing allure of confidence and style, while claiming to have your best interests at heart, and they speak with words of eloquence; but at the end of the day, there is no evidence of good intention. Concerning the complexities of life, they appear to be in possession of insurmountable comprehension; but under the microscope you will discover that their life is filled with sadness and pain, sickness and rain, anxiety and hypertension. The Fixer is not your friend.

The answers that you seek from man can instead be filled by the one who has a divine plan. Why consult human beings who are also lost, while you search for direction at any cost? Don't wait until you end up broke, busted and disgusted, having a wasted life, acquiring acquaintances who cannot be trusted; perpetually being surrounded by anxiety and strife. Then, when all of your resources are far spent, and you sit back and review while you lament, you begin to discover that all you have left is just a few pennies to spare. Don't wait until you've wasted your life's talents on people who didn't care, people with undiscovered dreams and unreleased potential. The company that you keep can be quite detrimental.

So arise from the scandalous affair that they present; no longer allow them into your life; move forward, repent. Bring yourself to the realization that there is greater in you than what exists within those who claim to possess the world.

Don't take detours in the pursuit of purpose. If you do, you will voluntarily forfeit divine instruction and be left by the wayside to settle for bootleg intervention. Don't embrace The Fixer. Why seek illumination from them who walk in darkness?

<u>SOLITUDE</u>

Sometimes the solitude is what I need; it's
where I breed the seed of creativity.
It's where I lock away from unproductive minds that try to lead me
astray, but it's also where I'm sometimes found in silent dismay.

But this safe haven of solitude is where I sometimes go to protect
others from my attitude. It's where I can chill, relax, consecrate, and
rejuvenate, instead of being rude. It's where the burden of the test can be
released and it's where I can find peace, and where I allow my anxiety
to decrease. For in the solitude, there seems to be a bit less stress; it's
where my sense of tranquility is at its best. It's where I can separate
from the rest, and forget about all the day's mess, in the solitude.

For too many minds cluttered together create a social atmosphere
that equates to bad weather. Because although great minds think
alike, unproductive minds cause great strife, and when the heat
rises, on each other they begin to strike. To me, that sounds
like such an unfulfilling, cantankerous life. Yet, so many of us
continue to surround ourselves with others who we do not trust,
even though we know they do not wish us the best. They wouldn't
mind if we chose to place our purpose on a shelf, as we aimlessly
with them exist in a state of unrest; for misery loves company.

But in the solitude, in the solitude you can be who you want
to be; you can make all your dreams a reality, and you can run
passionately in the direction of your destiny. But hey, I'm aware
that no man is an island; indeed, no man stands alone. But before
you proceed to take refuge in a friend when you're in need, and
walk with them hand in hand, take heed, and remember never to
stray away from your divine plan. Because at the end of the day, we
will all get our just pay, we can only reap what we have sown.

So never criticize the realm of the solitude, it is sometimes a threshing floor for your purpose. So while you stand alone, instead of wallowing in disgust, try instead to regain your focus. There is great mystery inside of thee; you are more than what the eyes meet. The inner person that we cannot see is a treasure chest of destiny. But the treasure can sometimes only be unlocked in the solitude. For this is where peace, contentment and creativity all drive on the same street; and like the instruments of a symphony, they all move to the same beat. So if you're searching for me, in the solitude is where I'll be, fulfilling my destiny, in the solitude.

CHAPTER 18

THE ENTOURAGE

During the days of growth and abundance, friends are a dime a dozen, or so it seems. However, the reality is that *people,* not *friends,* are a dime a dozen; that is of course when life is going well and there is something of value attached to your life.

Friends, in contrast, fall under an entirely different category. These are the individuals that remained with you when life seemingly brought you to your lowest state. While you existed in that dungeon, that valley of death and sorrow, these were the individuals who came alongside you and said, *"I'm with you my friend."* They held you and consoled you when the sorrows that you endured made you feel reproachable. They bore your pain; or rather, they would have if they could. At the very least, they empathized with you, existing in your presence although the reproach of your condition, from your perspective, seemed detestable.

They were your confidants when the addiction of sin had you strung out, feeling like you were about to lose your mind. It was these friends that came to you and said: *"Better days are coming, hold your head up; there is a light at the end of the tunnel. I'm with you; we'll get through this together."*

These are the ones who have earned the very distinguished title and can worthily be called, "friends." But the entourage is an interesting bunch, consisting of friend and foe, well-wisher and backbiter, faithful comrade and unscrupulous betrayer.

Amongst the entourage, you'll find those that are for you and those that are very passionately against you. Their facade is so embolden that they are willing to stand in pretence even in your presence, and dwell alongside you with the hopes of latching on to you; operating like a leech, sucking the very life out of you until this activity is no longer beneficial for them.

The entourage is not to be desired. If it exists, then run with it under the leading of the Spirit and the discipline of wisdom. But if it doesn't exist, don't seek after it. You don't need a multitude in order to be relevant. Don't wonder, *"Why is it that I've found myself in a place of solitude? Why am I alone in the season of great trial?"* Nor should you wonder, *"Where are my friends, and where is my support group?"* Don't ponder on these things, because it will only breathe discouragement and cloud your mind from the truth.

The truth is that although God often uses other individuals to help with the birthing of our purpose, there are also seasons when it is necessary for us to exist in the solitude for a while. It is there that God can begin to really deal with us on an intimate level. This meeting must occur through one-on-one conference, a face-to-face encounter; it is a personal and private assignation between you and the King. For this appointment, the entourage must be left behind. Therefore, God himself orchestrates it to be so, as He lifts us out from amongst those that crowded us and He summons us to the haven of His holy mountain alone.

> *"And when he had sent the multitudes away, he went up into a mountain apart to pray: and when the evening was come, he was there alone."*
> *(Matthew 14:23 KJV)*

CHAPTER 19

OPEN HEART SURGERY

It is from the corridors of His secret place that the Lord beckons us to come up higher. This private getaway is not to be taken for granted, because the Word of God teaches us that it is indeed a privilege to ascend into the holy hill of the Lord. To be found in His Holy Place is an awesome unmerited privilege that should be greatly appreciated and cherished. For, *"Who may ascend into the hill of the LORD? Or who may stand in His holy place?" (Psalm 24:3 NKJV)*

The question is asked in a rather rhetorical manner, because it is understood that the presence of God is so very holy that really no man can stand in God's presence based on his own merit or esteem. We must therefore greatly revere God's presence to the point that we count none worthy of standing in this place, but that which is covered by God. Of course God is indeed omnipresent, which means He is everywhere. So no matter where we go, technically by that definition, we are still in God's presence. But in this context it speaks of the Holy Place, the intimate corridors of the Lord in which we can be refreshed by the dew of His glory.

We don't deserve such a privilege, but it is granted to us through the awesome wonder of the grace of God. He embraces us with His never failing love and His wondrous mercy, as He invites us into His presence. It is for this reason that God orchestrated the tearing of the veil, which symbolized the mending of the breach between God and man; this breach being caused by sin and repaired by the redemptive blood of Jesus Christ.

The tearing of the veil was therefore a tearing away of the barrier that prevented us from entering into the promises of our heavenly Father. Sin created that barrier, Jesus became our bridge. He became our access. The veil was torn so that we may have free access to His presence.

Although salvation is free, it certainly came with a high cost. While we were dead in our sins, Jesus Christ voluntarily gave up his life as the sacrifice for our sins. That's an expensive transaction. Salvation could only be bought through the shed blood of Jesus Christ, and Jesus paid our debt in full. What an amazing God we serve!

Having knowledge of such grace, we should revere the communion that we experience amidst God's secret place. The blood of Jesus Christ was shed to enable us to have such peace, such comfort and contentment.

It is there, in the secret place of our King that the Lord begins to download revelations of mysteries into our very being, through the mainframe of our heart. *"Above all else, guard your heart, for everything you do flows from it." (Proverbs 4:23 NIV)*

It is through that spiritual download within the heart that we are granted free access to the strategies and principles that we must follow in order to accomplish our purpose. We would do well to live according to the design that God created for us, long before we were even given the breath of life.

> *"Call to me and I will answer you, and will tell you great and hidden things that you have not known." (Jeremiah 33:3 ESV)*

Inside the secret place, even the subconscious secrets of our own hearts are revealed to us, as we become completely naked before our King. It's because it is such an intimate encounter with our Counsellor, our Friend, that we can become completely naked before Him, void of all inhibition or pretence.

> *"He who dwells in the secret place of the Most High shall abide under the shadow of the Almighty." (Psalm 91:1 NKJV)*

This is why God calls us away from the crowd and into the solitude, so that we may be transparent before Him without fear of reproach. He leads us into the dark confines of solitude so that He may be the light we have been searching for. He is the light that is able to illuminate every dark crevice of our lives.

Before we can boldly walk out the principles God has given us, and begin to manifest our purpose, we must first deal with ourselves. We must initiate a thorough investigation of the inner man, the man behind the mask. We cannot ignore the man who is crying out to be healed, but who is also too ashamed to disrobe himself in front of the physician.

That wounded man will therefore remain with his ailment until his pain becomes more overwhelming than his pride. Jesus is calling this man before Him. The Lord Jesus Christ is indeed The Great Physician and He desires that none of us should perish. The Lord desires that all who find themselves in His presence will grab a hold of the virtue that He possesses and receive healing from every ailment or infirmity.

The Lord wants to remedy every deficiency existing in our emotional life, our spiritual man, our physical being, and even the instability of our finances. In the design of a loving Father, we are given principles that steer us towards stepping out of lack and working towards a prosperous life, that places the Lord at the centre of our motives.

In the obedience of God's design we comprehend that even the accumulation of our finances should be placed under submission to the Lord, understanding that it is God that enables us to obtain wealth to bring him glory.

> *"He fed you with manna in the wilderness, a food unknown to your ancestors. He did this to humble you and test you for your own good. He did all this so you would never say to yourself, 'I have achieved this wealth with my own strength and energy.'* [18] *Remember the LORD your God. He is the one who gives you power to be successful, in order to fulfill the covenant he confirmed to your ancestors with an oath." (Deuteronomy 8:16-18 NLT)*

It is in the mountain of His splendour, in the magnificent radiance of His glory that He heals us from such deficiencies and brings us to a place of wholeness. It is then that we become equipped to return to the battlefield, and take back all that the enemy has for us and begin to truly manifest our purpose.

How can we minister to others before we ourselves become healed? We would exist as individuals plagued with all manner of pestilence, while simultaneously trying to fulfill the role of physician to God's wounded soldiers. We may exist in that capacity for a while, but it won't be long before such practices may spell D.E.A.T.H for those whom we minister to, as well as ourselves.

DEGENERATE: *"Having lost the physical, mental, or moral qualities considered normal and desirable; showing evidence of decline."* – Oxford Dictionary.

When we become degenerate within the vein of our purpose, we become less effective in all that we do. Similar to the breakdown of the body, the breaking of the spirit affects our output. Our performance is diminished because we become weak within our mind and spirit, which ultimately causes a decline in our physical energy as well. The body responds to the instruction of the mind.

EXHAUSTED: *"Completely used used up; no longer productive as a result of being drained of resources." - Oxford Dictionary.*

In this state we begin to feel empty, out of steam, and completely fatigued. It is difficult to focus on purpose when you feel like you have no fuel left in the tank. It is hard to muster the strength to keep going when you feel like you have just given it your last ounce of effort. The body shuts down and the mind enters a process of overload, while your spirit becomes isolated and out of tune with its divine source.

APATHETIC: *"Showing or feeling no interest, enthusiasm, or concern." – Oxford Dictionary*

After the feeling of exhaustion sets in, the natural progression is to become withdrawn and indifferent to the needs of others. Here we begin to justify our feelings of disinterest under the umbrella of self-preservation. In the attempt to shelter ourselves from the shower of stress and external anxiety, we put up emotional walls of apathy that are used to obstruct anything that appears to threaten our peace of mind. But while attempting to block out the world, we also succeed in the process of incarcerating ourselves.

TRANSIENT: *"Lasting only for a short time; impermanent. Staying or working in a place for a short time only." - Oxford Dictionary*

When we are detached while trying to operate in our purpose, we become transient; because it is easy to lose our sense of commitment when we begin to feel disconnected. When we are disconnected, we begin to drift in the wind, like a branch cut off from its vine. When we are exhausted and apathetic, we tend to find more fault with our environment than we do with ourselves. We blame our circumstances on external forces, rather than taking responsibility of the consequences of our actions. In this season, we change churches frequently, or refuse to attend one any at all. When we do associate with a church family, we remain detached in a continual reluctance to bring our gifts to the house of the Lord so that we can be used by God corporately. We are always on the move, yet never really going anywhere. When we are transient we are in motion without progress.

HYPOCRITICAL: *"Saying that you have particular moral beliefs but behaving in a way that shows these are not sincere." –* *Cambridge Dictionary*

When we have lost the passion for our purpose, and we become degenerate, exhausted, apathetic and transient, we begin to appear to others as hypocritical. This is often an unfair assessment of our sincerity. It's not that we want to be hypocritical; but there are seasons when our faith and our reality eventually collide, and within those circumstances we must decide if we will believe what God says, or concede defeat. When our passion has been drained, accepting defeat seems logical. When we are disconnected, we place less emphasis on accountability. So our actions begin to contradict our values. We were once very zealous in the expression of those same values, but during the painful process of pursuing purpose, we sometimes become weary and we appear duplicitous.

At this juncture, we are flirting with a morbid expression of our spirituality. We are flirting with a type of spiritual death. It is a tragedy that is avoidable; yet many of us often become broken and weary, and we fall into this deep slumber of apathy. This calamity is common when we are wounded.

Purposeful resting and being burnt out isn't synonymous. Occasionally pulling away on a temporary basis to recuperate, retool and realign our focus, is totally acceptable; in fact, it is advisable. The contrasting tragedy occurs when we simply shut down due to exhaustion and no longer have the desire to continue.

That tragedy may occur simply because we have neglected our own healing process. That's a scary thought, but it's true. Would you mind having a doctor operate on you who happened to be attached to life support himself? You would probably object to that, as would I. We must therefore contend with the spirit of pride before we can truly be effective servants to God's people. It is ok to acknowledge when we are struggling, and it is ok to seek help.

This is not a licence to become intentionally inconsistent in our walk with Christ, nor is it a validation for a backsliding mentality. We are to remain steadfast in our progress throughout difficulty and turmoil, and indeed we should remain militantly grounded, even amidst our own personal struggles.

However, with that being said, even on the battlefield, wounded soldiers sometimes must retreat for medical treatment when needed. It is clearly understood that a wounded soldier is less effective in the time of battle, and may potentially cause more damage to himself and be more of a threat to his own army than that of the enemy. Therefore, there is a process of healing that must be endured.

Why do some of us refuse to seek healing when we know that we're struggling with our weakness and brokenness? Why is it that we deem it more desirable to hide our wounds beneath our military camouflage, instead of admitting that we are bleeding and in need of help?

As believers, some of us have convinced ourselves that spirituality equates to perfection, and that being wounded is synonymous to being defeated.

So in the attempt to hide our perceived defeat, we subsequently hide our wounds from others; but only to our own demise, resulting in the downfall of those who are looking to us to aid their strength.

My friend, God has already made provision for you and me. He is willing and waiting to heal us, if we would only allow Him to do so. But to do this, we must first be willing to step beyond our pride, our self-righteousness and the opinions of man, and lay our burdens on Him. As we lay our burdens on the Lord, let's recline on God's operation table, resting peaceably as He performs the process of healing in our mind, body and spirit.

> *"Is there no balm in Gilead? Is there no physician there? Why then has the health of the daughter of my people not been restored?" (Jeremiah 8:22 ESV)*

CHAPTER 20

<u>FILTHY RAGS</u>

Have you ever encountered an individual who exudes such an intoxicating stench of self-righteousness that you just wanted to run from their presence and hide? Someone so flattered by their own opinion of themselves that they can't even look in the mirror without blushing? If you're anything like me, when you come across such an individual, your dialogue would probably sound something like the following:

"Ok, we get it, you're very holy; that's wonderful. Bravo, congratulations, take a bow. As for the rest of us, who actually need exoneration on a daily basis, please allow me to say this, just remember that the holy land in which you currently reside was once a place of mystery for you as well. Yes, you too were once estranged from the country of flawlessness, and if the truth be told, you still are. You were once a wandering alien without moral citizenship. Everyone has a past; yes, even you."

So the next time you turn up your nose at a struggling individual, remember that even God's measure of grace is greater than his level of righteous indignation. So, who are you? Who am I to condemn another, when I stand in need of grace on a daily basis?

"Simon, Simon, Satan has asked to sift each
of you like wheat. But I have pleaded in prayer

for you, Simon, that your faith should not fail. So when you have repented and turned to me again, strengthen your brothers." (Luke 22: 31-32 NLT)

Now, we dare not minimize our legitimate responsibility to strive towards a mark of holiness. As believers, we most certainly do have *A Call to Holy Living.*

"So think clearly and exercise self-control. Look forward to the gracious salvation that will come to you when Jesus Christ is revealed to the world. So you must live as God's obedient children. Don't slip back into your old ways of living to satisfy your own desires. You didn't know any better then. But now you must be holy in everything you do, just as God who chose you is holy. For the Scriptures say, "You must be holy because I am holy." (1 Peter 1:13-16 NLT)

So of course, by all means, we should embrace holiness as the standard of living. That being said, we should also be cognizant that our own righteousness, our greatest attempt at individual holiness, at best, is filthy in the sight of God. Our only claim to a genuine state of holiness can only be achieved when we allow ourselves to be clothed in the purity of a Holy God.

"And all of this is a gift from God, who brought us back to himself through Christ. And God has given us this task of reconciling people to him. For God was in Christ, reconciling the world to himself, no longer counting people's sins against them. And he gave us this wonderful message of reconciliation. So we are Christ's

ambassadors; God is making his appeal through us. We speak for Christ when we plead, "Come back to God!" For God made Christ, who never sinned, to be the offering for our sin, so that we could be made right with God through Christ."
(2 Corinthians 5:18-21 NLT)

It is with this understanding that all pride and self-righteousness should be dispelled. We are nothing without the grace of God. We are, at best, creatures of decaying morality and we are unable to sustain ourselves. Even amidst our own proclaimed rules of integrity, we still inevitably fail, we constantly miss the mark.

But, the book of Jude declares, ***"Now unto him that is able to keep you from falling, and to present you faultless before the presence of his glory with exceeding joy, to the only wise God our Saviour, be glory and majesty, dominion and power, both now and ever. Amen." (Jude 1:24-25 KJV)***

FIRE THE EMISSARY

I see a man looking right at me, but I don't seem to recognize. I see his face, his eyes, his nose, his lips; but all seem like a disguise. I hear the words this man speaks, and the echo they make seem rather unique. I then look closer into the mirror and begin to look deeper at his picture. I begin to comprehend that the man I see is sometimes who I pretend to be; very debonair and presentable, but inside sometimes feeling detestable.

I don't know if you've ever been there, being torn inside but a smile you continue to wear; feeling like you've been to the brink and are now hanging on by a thread. You sometimes feel like your purpose and focus have been either lost or left for dead.

Yet, others continue to pull as they draw strength from you; not realizing that your strength is lacking and also needs to be made new. They tell you of their burdens, their trials and their fears. They tell you of their failures & their shortcomings, on you they shed their tears.

Yet, the internal groaning that you utter is seemingly never heard or understood. So you fold within yourself, frustrated, even though you know it's working for your good. There is none to hear your cry, no shoulder on which to lean; so you continue to wear the disguise, always being present, but never really being seen. For the image they see is sometimes like a representative that you've sent. He goes ahead of you, exhibiting flawlessness and perfection; at least, that is your intent. Yet the real you would sometimes lag behind and hide, masking his blemishes. Not wanting to exhibit any show of imperfection, so this form of camouflage he cherishes.

But beneath it all you grow weary and become irritated by all the self-driven pretence. You become tired of being a distributor of counsel, yet never receiving any recompense. But, how can you ever be replenished if you continue to pretend that all is well? You can never receive help if not even God holds your

115

trust, none of your issues do you wish to tell. But I challenge you to remove the disguise, and no longer exist as that old image in the mirror. Instead, open yourself to the reality of life. We are imperfect and are sometimes given to blunder. Sometimes we are at the doorsteps of our breakthrough, but because of pride, our deliverance we repeatedly hinder.

But this is now a dawning of a new day; I challenge you to dismiss your ambassador. You're no longer in need of an emissary, transparency you should now restore. Why do we feel like our righteousness is indicative of a life lived in perfection? When we know our own righteousness is as filthy rags; we stand only by His redemption. For by the grace of God we are clothed in the righteousness of Christ. We are covered by His salvation. No need for self-righteousness, His blood has sufficed. So in this knowledge we release all our inhibition. We recognize that the pretence of perfection has been an awful tradition.

There is a freedom in transparency, a certain reward for being real. There is a release in simply being truthful concerning the emotions that you feel. No pretence, no camouflage, no ambassador, no emissary. The man you see in front of you is now the real man inside of me.

CHAPTER 21

<u>BEYOND THE VEIL</u>

I once went through a long season when I allowed my trials to become so very overwhelming that I locked away from my only source of help. I locked away from my relationship with Christ. I became bitter and began pouting, thinking that I deserved more out of life. If the truth be told, I would have to say that I allowed this to happen at numerous points during the early stages of my Christian walk. But specifically in that particular season of immaturity, I believed that the Almighty God, the King of Kings, somehow owed me something.

It was in this ignorance that I began running in the opposite direction of my purpose. I was chasing after dreams and ambitions that were not ordained by the Lord, and then wondering why those self-motivated dreams weren't working out. Having a passion for my carnal appetites but not having a passion after God. But then He spoke to me in my spirit and I recognized the message that I needed to hear from him; He said, *"Return to me, I long to fill that gap that you have created in your life."*

It was in that moment of truth that I repented for placing so many others within the place that God belongs. I had removed the Lord from His rightful place in my life and attempted to fill the gap with others. In my own quest for companionship, I had relinquished the most important relationship, my relationship with Christ.

117

In so doing, in an attempt to combat loneliness, I had searched externally for others to be companions. But in that process, I had denied the most important friend who incidentally exists inside of me. The Lord has continually proven to be a friend within me. During those times, He desired nothing more than to fill that gap of loneliness and to fill that gap of emptiness within me, with His presence instead of being incarcerated within the mental prison of my limitations.

The Lord is our portion and our provision. As He did with me, God can and He will help you to empty your mind of all selfish agenda and remove from you all of your carnal motives. He will grant you the spiritual eyes to see beyond your current circumstance, and you will therefore be able to passionately seek His face and fulfill your purpose.

It is through the eyes of the Spirit that we can see the full brilliance of His glory. It is when the Lord clothes us in His righteousness, and covers us in His salvation that we are able to truly see Him for who He is. It almost appears that through drawing nearer to the Lord, a cloak of revelation is thrown around us, and miraculously, we are granted the insight to see Jesus for who He is.

He gives us armour that evidently does more than just protect us in battle; I would argue that it also changes our perspective as well. It's under the breastplate of righteousness and under the helmet of salvation that the wisdom of God is revealed, and our heart is transformed into His likeness.

It is now time to cast away every carnal motive. It is in this season that we should ask God to wash our hands from walking in the desires and weaknesses of the flesh, and ask the Lord to empty us. We have need of Him to remove from us the things that we have placed upon God's throne, and ask the Lord Jesus Christ to fill our lives with His presence.

The Lord longs to fill the gap in your life. He longs to be the only one living at your altar; the only one sitting on the throne as King in your life. But we have allowed so many others to lead us, and subsequently they have inevitably led us astray. They have led us right into a dungeon of despair, right into a place of neglect and discontent; because none other belongs on this throne but God. No one else can fill that gap in your life but God.

Young man, the girlfriend who you hold so dearly to your heart, cannot be your source. Young lady, the boyfriend who you believe to be your world, must not be your focus. The wife or husband can't fill this void. The six figure bank account is really nice, but even that, by itself, can't do it.

That gap will continue to grow and get deeper until it consumes away our entire being, unless we allow God to fill it and return as the ruler who sits on the throne of our hearts. The Lord desires to be *governor* of our lives, but He will not be a tyrant, He must be elected by our free will.

> **"You shall have no other gods before me. You shall not make for yourself an image in the form of anything in heaven above or on the earth beneath or in the waters below. You shall not bow down to them or worship them; for I, the LORD your God, am a jealous God, punishing the children for the sin of the parents to the third and fourth generation of those who hate me."** *(Exodus 20:3-5 NIV)*

You might be saying at this point, *"Well, I don't by any means, HATE the Lord and I don't practice idol worship, so thanks for the advice...but I think I'm good."* But in our daily practices, some of us have allowed our own agendas to sit on the steps of the altar of sacrifice. Therefore, we entertain living distractions that really should be killed and placed upon the altar of God, as we bring them to the Lord as sacrifice so that He may consume them once and for all. It isn't only your body that should be presented as a *living sacrifice* before God. All unhealthy distractions to our purpose should be brought to the feet of the Lord and submitted as our sacrifice as we submit ourselves to the will of the Lord. When we submit our lives under the Glory of the Lord and bring those distractions to Him, those distractions that have become idols can then be consumed amidst the fire of His purification.

Sadly, instead, we have allowed that which should be rendered unto God to sit at the crevices of our heart, unburned and unrestrained; and those distractions remain alive. In our neglect, we have even allowed them to crawl upon the governing throne of our mind. They have taken the place of control and instruction in our lives, the place where God should be. These uninhibited things that should be offered as sacrifices have been running about upon the altar within some of us, and have not been surrendered under the hand of God.

These distractions have now grown and have taken up such a place of authority that they have even become as gods within your mind and your spirit. They have taken such a role of authority that the idea of giving them up now seems virtually impossible.

These retained habits once existed in a state of infancy, but now they have grown to become monstrous appetites that dictate to your mind which passions it is that you should pursue.

The apostle Paul recognized this within himself when he stated, *"I find then a law, that, when I would do good, evil is present with me." (Romans 7:21 KJV)*

Many times, in attempts to echo the words of Paul, some of us inadvertently misquote this scripture and instead of the above, we say, *"when I wish to do good, evil **presents itself**."* Which is not only unbiblical, it's also technically impossible. Contrary to what the theatrical presentation on the cinemas of Hollywood portray, *evil* does not roam about in a disembodied state of matter while seeking out an opportunity to manifest havoc, and **"present itself."** Surely the devil is evil, and he certainly does roam about in the realm of the spirit world, but even he needs a body in which to become manifest. *"Stay alert! Watch out for your great* *enemy, the devil. He prowls around like a roaring lion, looking for someone to devour." (1 Peter 5:8 NLT)*

Therefore, the correct extract of the scripture states that *"evil is present **with** me."*

If I would be bold enough to offer my interpretation of that verse, I would dare to read the verse as follows, *"When I would to do good, evil is present **within** me"*

It is only when we allow the enemy to step within our mind that we give the devil an open door. Of course, as blood washed believers, the devil has no *habitation* within us; he has no legal right to dwell on the real estate of our heart. We are sealed by the Holy Spirit and therefore our house is not up for sale; there is no vacancy in our spiritual home, we belong to God. But with all of that being true, sometimes our actions allow the devil to gain access to the corridors of our mind. It is then that he is able to operate through us and even against us by our own authority that we have bequeathed to him. It is because of this reason that the devil is able to rule within the various areas of our lives. *"But every man is tempted, when he is drawn away of his own lust, and enticed." (James 1:14 KJV)*

This is why Paul recognized that we are required to die daily, that we may therefore mortify the carnal agenda of the flesh, so that we may be able to live by the spirit, sober-minded and focused; so that we may see clearly to dispel all manner of evil away from our vision and our purpose. We must therefore bring our bodies, our flesh, and our carnal desires to God daily so that He may consume them on the altar of sacrifice.

Today we have been granted direct access to God because of the shed blood of Jesus Christ; therefore, tearing the veil of partition in the temple, which once separated God and man and caused us to have need of a high priest to offer atonement for our sins.

But today, we can have deep intimacy with God. We can go beyond the veil and commune with Him face to face.

>*"Therefore, brethren, having boldness to enter the Holiest by the blood of Jesus, by a new and living way which He consecrated for us, through the veil, that is, His flesh, and having a High Priest over the house of God, let us draw near with a true heart in full assurance of faith, having our hearts sprinkled from an evil conscience and our bodies washed with pure water." (Hebrews 10:19:22 NKJV)*

It is only then that we are able to be healed, and only after we are healed can we be effective warriors on the battlefield.

CHAPTER 22

A TIME FOR WAR

Strategy, strategy, strategy, this is the best way to win a war; by devising a plan, developing an excellent course of action concerning how an enemy may be attacked and successfully conquered. Even *"More-Than-Conquerors"* need strategies concerning how they will conquer. Emotion and passion alone cannot, and will not win the war. The enemy has declared war against you. He has very brazenly, very aggressively attacked your purpose, your destiny and your gifting; it's time to send a message that you will not be defeated in the pursuit of your purpose. However, simply retaliating isn't enough. We must designate a time to strategize. If you have no plan of action, consequently you have already planned to fail. A failure to plan is a very foolproof plan of defeat.

One of the most infamous terrorist attacks made against the residents of The United States was done by the intentional plummeting of two large planes into the two buildings of The World Trade Centre. This occurred in the city of Manhattan, New York on September 11, 2001. These two very tall buildings, known as the Twin Towers, which formerly stood erect in the city of Manhattan, were utterly demolished by the impact and explosion of the aircrafts that were guided to intentionally collide into them. It was said that the individuals who flew those planes were a part of an elaborate terrorist plot against the residence of the United States. This occurrence was a devastating attack on not only the nation of America, but it also significantly affected the world's economy.

To communicate the occurrence of this tragic emergency, the news bulletins continued to run across the screens, repeatedly displaying the visually recorded captions of devastation. So, as the world watched while the magnificence of the Twin Towers was brought down to mere rubbles, and as the lives within the structures were taken away prematurely, the leader of the nation had to now make a decision. It was decided that it was then time for war.

"To everything there is a season, and a time to every purpose under the heaven… a time to love, and a time to hate; a time of war, and a time of peace." (Ecclesiastes 3:1, 8 NKJV)

The devastating event that occurred on September 11, 2001 is now known worldwide simply as 9/11. There were and still are many controversial opinions about the occurrence of the 9/11 catastrophe. However, the purpose of this analogy isn't necessarily to support or refute either opinion; but instead, it is merely to conclude that when a nation is attacked, the leadership of that land is left with the task of making decisions. Those decisions, whatever they may be, will determine the state of national security that will exist in that land thereafter.

In like manner, the enemy has attacked the towers of your purpose. He has sent fiery darts in your direction and has targeted your vision. He has sent his imps to wrap shackles around the limbs of your gifting, to cripple your momentum. What is your next course of action? Will you retaliate? Good! I'm sure the answer to that is "yes." But even in your newfound passion, you must not proceed unless you have a strategy; because even in the midst of war, there are rules of engagement. There is a certain type of protocol even in the midst of war.

You don't just get up and fight emotionally and spontaneously. That would result in chaos and possibly self-destruction. The actions of the enemy must be weighed and critiqued, *"Lest Satan should get an advantage of us: for we are not ignorant of his devices." (2 Corinthians 2:11 KJV)*

So let us not be in any way ignorant of the enemy's schemes. It is in this season of strategizing, this season of planning, that we also begin to update our inventory. We evaluate our stock of ammunition and determine which weapons, which angle of attack will be appropriate for the battle ahead.

In August of 1945 the world witnessed another devastating attack against fellow human beings. But this attack didn't come from unknown terrorist; instead, this retaliating attack came from an organized, tactical assignment ordered and executed by the United States Air Force. This attack was one that almost utterly decimated the Japanese cities of Hiroshima and Nagasaki.

After the bombs were dropped, the effects of the chemicals weren't discriminating. Both soldier and civilian became victims of the detrimental effects of the atomic bombs. Neither senior citizens nor toddlers were exempt from this attack. The mother that tucked her child away moments before, and also the child that slept peaceably in the comfort of his crib, were both consumed by the glare of the radiant lights and the heat that was produced by the chemical blasts. Their flesh was consumed, in but a moment. Their bones became brittle and their limbs became feeble, as their lives were extinguished in a horrific, excruciating fashion. As for the rest who somehow managed to survive the attack, they were left deformed, incapacitated, with radiation sickness, traumatically affected, and burnt beyond recognition. Some became victims of cancerous effects long after the bombs had fallen.

The chemical attack on Hiroshima and Nagasaki occurred so many years ago, but the effects of this act of war are still very tangible today. Many of the survivors of that chemical attack are still suffering today in some way.

That day of devastation was also another time of war, and a decision had to be made concerning the strategy, the type of ammunition, and the time of attack that would be the appropriate measure during that military strike. The combined death toll of the attacks on Hiroshima and Nagasaki, including the deaths caused by the after effects of the bombing, was estimated to be over 200,000 people.

So a decision was made and 200,000 people died as a result. A decision was made and a large portion of a nation was brought to ruins. A decision was made and young babies, old women, young men and old men alike were sent to meet their Maker.

This critique is by no means an endorsement on the actions taken in Hiroshima. It was a horrific time that the world witnessed and many innocent lives were lost. It's very sad, and very demoralizing, and indeed there are really no winners in such devastating scenarios. No matter which side is victorious, it can arguably be professed that the act of war takes a piece of our humanity away when we have to resort to taking the life of another human being.

These pieces of history were extracted to solidify the point that strategy is imperative when engaging in war. Similarly, in the spiritual warfare that we fight daily, it is also quite important to not only be mindful of our strategy, but we must also be quite cognizant of which weapons we use.

Some may say that the devastating loss of innocent civilian lives that occurred at Hiroshima and Nagasaki was unavoidable and is simply a normal, inevitable consequence in the horrible reality of war. That may or may not be true; we'll save that argument for the military philosophers. But what we will discuss is what happens in everyday life when we fight with the wrong weapons. It is presumed that many, if not all of the "superpower nations" of the world are quite possibly in possession of some nuclear weapons. That in itself presents a huge problem. If one day all the nations of the world were to engage in a world war and the decision is made to use such nuclear weapons in attempts to "fight fire with fire," wouldn't that ultimately mean the complete destruction of the entire world as we know it?

From this we recognize that it is possible to fight the right war with the wrong weapons. Although the purpose of war is to conquer, kill and utterly destroy the enemy, sometimes the simplest truth is the most logical theory. Fighting a war in that manner would seem to defeat the purpose, if during the process, the attacker is also ultimately destroyed alongside his enemy due to a lack of wisdom.

Therefore, when we fight spiritual wars against our adversary the devil, let us be tactical in our approach. Let us not run passionately without having a plan. Let us not fight battles with impure motives. Let us not harm the innocent in our attempt of achieving our goals. Let's be mindful of the blows that we inflict and the stones that we throw, so as to ensure that in our fight against the enemy, we don't fail to recognize our real target.

Many times while claiming to be engaging in spiritual warfare, we lose our focus while being overwhelmed by ungodly motives, and we allow those motives to become Commander-In-Chief. Such actions cause harm to innocent bystanders, who are sometimes even our loved ones. In the long run, this consequently produces self-inflicted emotional harm, all in the name of spiritual warfare.

IN THE TRENCHES

In the everyday battles of life: On the job, in the educational system, and hey, let's face it, even within the church, we must be mindful of the weapons that we use. While we believe we're fighting the enemy, the enemy often sits back and watches us attack our spouses, our children, and our church congregants, under the camouflage of spiritual warfare.

It seems incongruous to engage in spiritual warfare while fighting with the weapons of our flesh. It is because of such tainted strategies that a man who is fed up with the oppressive environment at work, tired of being oppressed on the job, tired of being dealt meaningless tasks that have no promise of promotion, and tired of being disrespected by his superiors at work, goes home and brutalizes his wife because dinner wasn't ready on time.

It is for this same reason that his son, who procrastinates in taking out the garbage that evening, gets slapped in a quick and harsh punishment for a simple and slight blunder. This man, who professes to be a born again, tongue-talking, Holy Ghost filled believer, has raged war on his family and then isolates himself to sit on his porch at the end of the day with a very cold bottle of Heineken. He remains in his solitude until he is almost half-way through his second case of six-pack, because he says he needs that to "calm his nerves." He then begins to ponder on the day's events as he utters, *"I can't handle all of this stress, look what the enemy made me do, the devil is a liar."* This he says, as he proceeds to throw back his head while he empties another bottle down his throat.

Well brother Jim-Bob, *in this situation*, I dare say to you that the devil isn't a liar. You're simply walking in the flesh, and as you continue to walk in the flesh, you continue to fight your battles with the weapons of the flesh; while reaping the results thereof.

The devil didn't *make* Jim-Bob abuse his wife, his flesh did. The devil didn't force him to behave harshly to his child, his flesh did.

Which weapons are you using to fight with? Be quite careful, because if you use the wrong ones, you can cause damage to those around you that you love. Innocent people crossing your path will be hurt because you are fighting with the wrong weapons. Your ministry can potentially be aborted because you're fighting with the wrong weapons. Your reputation as a devout Christian on the job can be tarnished because you're fighting with the wrong weapons. Which weapons are you fighting with?

> *"For the weapons of our warfare are not of the flesh but have divine power to destroy strongholds."* (2 Corinthians 10:4 ESV)

THE MINEFIELD

As spirit-filled believers, the devil cannot make us do anything. However, he can attempt to cloud our judgement so that we might choose to make unwise decisions. Those decisions could affect the direction of our destiny, if we allow the devil to have such access.

The enemy therefore will attempt to place some strongholds on your ministry; he will try to place strongholds on your vision, your joy and your peace. The devil has attacked your destiny and has strategically situated some time bombs on the road along your pursuit of purpose. He has intentionally placed strongholds especially on the passion that you have within to fulfill your purpose and destiny. But now that you know, once you've identified the stronghold, and once you've found each shackle and ticking bomb of destruction in your life, break them off, shake them off and disengage them accordingly.

It is only through spiritual wisdom that some bombs will be diffused in your life. It is by this spiritual wisdom that you gain the discernment to locate those bombs that are laid amidst the minefields of life, before they explode in your face and bring death to your purpose. So find those shackles, those strongholds, shake them off, break them off and then continue to attack the enemy at full force. But before you attack, make sure that you know your strategy.

> *"And it shall come to pass in that day, that his burden shall be taken away from off*

> *thy shoulder, and his yoke from off thy neck,*
> *and the yoke shall be destroyed because of the*
> *anointing." (Isaiah 10:27 KJV)*

The yokes, the shackles and the strongholds are all destroyed because of the weapon of the anointing. It is with this weapon that we should fight. The weapons of the anointing, the word and of prayer will bolster our confidence during the battle; we know that through God, victory has already been granted. We merely need to walk in the Spirit as we continue to fight militantly on the battlefield, pursuing our purpose with great passion.

It is because of the anointing that the enemy will crumble. It was because of the God-given authority that the walls of Jericho fell. The people of Israel were given an unusual strategy; this army was told to simply march. They were told by the Lord to march around the territory of the enemy; during this time, they were to say nothing and do absolutely nothing for six consecutive days. There were six days of silence, but then on the seventh day of marching, they were commissioned to give a shout; on the seventh day they were instructed to make a noise of victory and blow the trumpets that they had been given, as a declaration of war and a simultaneous proclamation of triumph.

> *"Then the LORD said to Joshua, 'See, I have*
> *delivered Jericho into your hands, along with*
> *its king and its fighting men. March around*
> *the city once with all the armed men; do this for*
> *six days. Have seven priests carry trumpets of*
> *rams' horns in front of the ark. On the seventh*
> *day, march around the city seven times, with the*
> *priests blowing the trumpets. When you hear*
> *them sound a long blast on the trumpets, have*
> *all the people give a loud shout; then the wall of*

> *the city will collapse and the people will go up,*
> *every man straight in.'" (Joshua 6:2-5 NIV)*

So on the seventh day, the children of Israel did as they were told by the Lord; they echoed a loud shout, and the priests blew the trumpets as the Lord said they should, and the walls of Jericho tumbled. But what is important to note is that the walls fell because of the authority that the people possessed. The children of Israel were now walking in a Godly authority that was granted to them, simply because they were walking in obedience to the Word of the Lord and His command.

Sometimes we miss great accomplishments, and lose both trivial as well as significant battles, because of disobedience. Despite the fact that victory has already been predetermined by our Father, at times we still lose, only because we fail to execute simple assignments. There was nothing complicated or sophisticated about the Lord's instructions; all He said to do was march and make some noise. It couldn't have been any more straightforward than that. Quite often, the Lord's instructions to us are also just as simple, *"No, that companion isn't right for you, wait for another."* But there are so many times when some of us have heard those same words, and yet we chose to turn a deaf ear, to find out years later that if we only listened we could have saved ourselves from many years of hurt, emotional abuse, discontentment and overall misery; if we only followed the Lord's instructions, we could have avoided such hurt, which was caused by the companion whom some of us pleaded with the Lord to keep. Some of us often go back to God to negotiate, so that he may fix our lives according to our own desires instead of according to His will. We often try to conduct this bargaining exercise, even though we know the Lord already said, "No."

Or maybe the Lord might challenge us concerning our level of submission and very specifically say, *"My child, today I want you to increase your offering by doubling the amount of your usual tithe as a sacrificial offering unto me, so that I may show forth my provision in this season."* To which some of us would respond in the same manner as Jim-Bob responded earlier, "The devil is a liar!" No Jimmy, that isn't the devil, that's just Jesus training you to rise above the level of lack and financial dependency, and exist in a realm of faith and submission under the leading of the Master's hand. This we can do in assurance that we will not lack for anything; because the Word of the Lord tells us that He will indeed supply all our needs.

> **"And this same God who takes care of me will supply all your needs from his glorious riches, which have been given to us in Christ Jesus." (Philippians 4:19 NLT)**

So as any good soldier, the Lord desires that we also be submissive to the general of His army. If we can be humbled under the leading of the Spirit, we will have no problem grasping the fact that the reason the walls of Jericho fell on the seventh day, wasn't simply because the people shouted. But instead, the walls fell because their shout was accompanied by their God-given authority. If we can comprehend that, then we will also understand that a shout in itself which is void of the anointing, will render no results. It will merely be noise in the ears of the enemy. But we will do no real damage to the enemy's kingdom if we attack him with our carnal weapons. Even acts of spirituality can become carnal when they are done outside of the anointing.

> *"If I speak in the tongues of men and of angels, but have not love, I am only a resounding gong or a clanging cymbal. If I have the gift of prophecy and can fathom all mysteries and all knowledge, and if I have a faith that can move mountains, but have not love, I am nothing. If*

I give all I possess to the poor and surrender my body to the flames, but have not love, I gain nothing." (1 Corinthians 13:1-3 NIV)

It is therefore in the Spirit and by faith that we fight this battle. Let us fight, let us fight violently and vehemently; but let us fight by devising a strategy. The strategy is simple: Be fed by the Word of God daily, and daily live prayerfully and commit to a surrendered life to Christ; the Lord will take care of the rest.

"Fight the good fight for the true faith. Hold tightly to the eternal life to which God has called you, which you have declared so well before many witnesses." (1Timothy 6:12 NLT)

CHAPTER 23

<u>SMOKE SCREEN</u>

Amidst the heat of the fight, the enemy sometimes attempts to counterfeit the actions and tactics of God. The enemy recognizes that God fights on our behalf by using strategies that are made manifest through his people in the natural realm, while He continuously breaks down barriers in spiritual dimensions. So the enemy desires to operate in a similar manner, but of course for an evil agenda.

Often we will find that some situations in our natural realities are a reflection of what is occurring in the spiritual realm. Knowing this truth, Satan attempts to use intricately designed strategies when fighting against us. The devil attempts to confuse us in the midst of the battle. In fact, he does this so well that sometimes we forget which war we are fighting. He places a smoke screen before our eyes that works like a form of *spiritual tear gas*. This causes us to be blinded by the confusion of our trials and the confusion of life's daily turmoil, until we forget our purpose and subsequently abandon our mission.

When this happens, our vision is smeared and we can no longer see ahead of us. Therefore, we become discouraged by the uncertainty that is created by the darkness of the situation. Under that type of attack it seems easiest to simply pack it in, look out for *"Numero Uno"* and leave the battlefield in an act of desertion.

> *"To illustrate the point further, Jesus told them this story: "A man had two sons. The younger son told his father, 'I want my share of your estate now before you die.' So his father agreed to divide his wealth between his sons.*
>
> *A few days later this younger son packed all his belongings and moved to a distant land, and there he wasted all his money in wild living..."*
> *(Luke 15:11-13 NLT)*

Like this prodigal son, some of us got sidetracked and lost our vision of the big picture. We were blinded by temporary circumstances and were therefore led to make decisions that were contrary to the will of God. We chose a road that seemed to bring immediate gratification, all because we were being led by carnal passions. We were led by the desires to please flesh and the desire to please selfish appetites. We knew what we wanted and we wanted it, "now!"

However, what we wanted and what we needed weren't always synonymous, and so the smoke screen went up again. You were led deeper into the dungeon of hopelessness as the nights became darker, and even during the days there hung a cloud of darkness. Such darkness was so overwhelming that it almost seemed as if there was a perpetual eclipse of the revelation that once illuminated your life. Because of the perpetual darkness of your situation, you just couldn't think straight, couldn't function, and couldn't focus on anything because your vision was so very foggy; totally marred by the smoke screen that the enemy threw at you.

It's in such darkness that the passion for our purpose begins to diminish. The fight becomes meaningless and irrelevant. We can no longer feel the motivation to press on, and it was during such experiences when some of us caved in and gave in to temporal passions. We gave in to our physical needs and our carnal ambitions. But hope in this situation depends on the resurrection of our passion, our Godly passion; this passion when ignited within us will be the burning fire that fuels our spiritual engines, and enables our pursuit on the road to destiny and purpose.

CHAPTER 24

<u>BURNING WITH PASSION</u>

Passion is an interesting element of the human construct. Passion in the context of this subject is the drive that an individual has to fulfill the call of God on his/her life. It is the desire that pushes one to achieve his or her purpose. It is the motivation that fuels the fire to our ambitions. But passion can be either good or bad, depending on the motive of our desires. Those motives will determine the type of fruit that we will reap.

There are various types of passion; among them are: *Intellectual Passion*, the desire for knowledge, the need to know, and the search for reason. This is the type of passion that causes us to prodigalize our savings, seeking infinite levels of degrees and certifications that have absolutely nothing to do with our purpose. By no means is that statement an indictment against the pursuit of education. As an educator myself, it would be irresponsible of me to imply that education shouldn't be pursued. Instead, what I am saying is that simply having passion without having direction is dangerous. It causes us to waste time and energy, and indeed, sometimes we do waste money on the wrong things, while having good intentions in the pursuit of knowledge.

But on the contrary, this same *intellectual passion* when directed correctly is the passion that causes us to continually yearn for the revelation of the unsearchable mysteries of God.

> *"Unto me, who am less than the least of all saints, is this grace given, that I should preach among the Gentiles the unsearchable riches of Christ." (Ephesians 3:8 KJV)*

"The riches of Christ" are *"unsearchable"* because these riches speak of spiritual mysteries that can only be unlocked through revelation. We cannot comprehend them solely by our carnal intellect. These mysteries far supersede our logical or cognitive construct, and it is only through the mind of Christ that we may comprehend them. But it is through our passion and our desire that God opens our limited minds, and illuminates our vision so that we may see and comprehend the mysteries of His Kingdom.

> *"Moreover the word of the L*ord *came to Jeremiah a second time, while he was still shut up in the court of the prison, saying, "Thus says the L*ord *who made it, the L*ord *who formed it to establish it (the L*ord *is His name): 'Call to Me, and I will answer you, and show you great and mighty things, which you do not know.'"* (Jeremiah 33:1-3 NKJV)

There must be a question before there is an answer. There must be a searching before there is a revelation. The Lord longs to unlock great mysteries and bring before us the truth concerning even the unsearchable things of God. It is when we seek Him that He begins to illuminate these truths that can only be seen through the eyes of His spirit.

CHAPTER 25

THE CHASE

*"As the deer longs for streams of water, so I
long for you, O God." (Psalm 42:1 NLT)*

It is the intense search, the fervent desire, the persistent longing, and the sincere need for God that gets his attention.

Arguably, it could be suggested that Jacob had such an intense passion in his personal pursuit for truth. It was for this reason that Jacob had a divine experience that would change the way he saw himself for the rest of his life.

*"And He said, "Your name shall no longer be
called Jacob, but Israel; for you have struggled
with God and with men, and have prevailed."
(Genesis 32:28 NKJV)*

It is said that Jacob wrestled with the Lord and prevailed. Did Jacob prevail because he was greater in stature, greater in strength or greater in power than God? Obviously neither of those suggestions is even remotely truthful. Such an interpretation would be profane.

It is most commonly accepted that Jacob prevailed because God was touched by his persistence. Jacob prevailed because God knew that Jacob's passion for his purpose was greater than the fear he may have felt in the midst of that circumstance. There he stood, wrestling with a higher being, a greater power than himself, but his desire was so great, and his passion was so potent that he was drunken by the pursuit of the truth. It was in this pursuit that he found not only a revelation of God, Jacob also found himself. Jacob found a new identity because he dared to pursue God.

What will you find when you begin to put aside the fear of your circumstance? What great mysteries are waiting for you that are yet to be revealed simply because you have not yet pursued them? Run after God, search for Him with your whole heart, and you will find Him.

> **"Then Jacob asked, saying, *"tell me your name, I pray."* And He said, "Why is it that you ask about my name?" And He blessed him there. So Jacob called the name of the place Peniel:** *"For I have seen God face to face, and my life is preserved."* **(Genesis 32:29-30 NKJV)**

Jacob's bold pursuit of truth was similar to the pursuit that Moses embarked on when he ascended into a strange mountain and was met by God in the form of a burning bush. You see, you have to go where you have never gone before in order to experience the extraordinary. Sometimes that truth is seen figuratively and sometimes it is literal. Sometimes you simply need to change your atmosphere in order to position yourself to receive what God has set aside for you in the midst of His glory. You will find your purpose inside of His glory. You will find the path of your calling in the midst of seeking the Lord. He will not give His glory to another. You will therefore only find true success when you empty yourself of your own agenda and make God your agenda, and relinquish all glory to Him. All glory belongs to God. Upon doing so, the radiance of your purpose will shine brightly, illuminated by the glistening reflection of His glory.

So Moses ascended into the mountain and encountered God. It is there, through the passion that was stirred up inside of Moses that Moses pleaded to be blessed with the privilege of seeing God's face. But instead, God hid Moses in the cleft of the rock and allowed only His presence to pass by Moses.

> *"But He said, "You cannot see My face; for no man shall see Me, and live." And the LORD said, "Here is a place by Me, and you shall stand on the rock. So it shall be, while My glory passes by, that I will put you in the cleft of the rock, and will cover you with My hand while I pass by. Then I will take away My hand, and you shall see My back; but My face shall not be seen.""* (Exodus 33:20-23 NKJV)*

If that is true, if indeed no man can see God and live, then what did Job mean when he testified the following? *"And after my skin has been thus destroyed, yet in my flesh I shall see God." (Job 19:26 ESV)* Job spoke prophetically of the resurrection of the saints, believing that after this temporary tabernacle is dissolved, the dead in Christ shall rise, and on that day we shall see God. Concerning the concept of "seeing" God, Job's confidence rested in the eternal.

Here's yet another scripture that points towards this glorious day when we will be transformed from our temporal realities to a new life beyond the gates of eternity.

> *"But let me reveal to you a wonderful secret. We will not all die, but we will all be transformed! It will happen in a moment, in the blink of an eye, when the last trumpet is blown. For when the trumpet sounds, those who have died will*

be raised to live forever. And we who are living will also be transformed. For our dying bodies must be transformed into bodies that will never die; our mortal bodies must be transformed into immortal bodies.

Then, when our dying bodies have been transformed into bodies that will never die, this Scripture will be fulfilled: "Death is swallowed up in victory. O death, where is your victory? O death, where is your sting?"" (1Corinthians 15:50-55 NLT)

Paul was referring to what mankind would become in our glorified body. But this scripture makes no reference of seeing the face of God on this side of life. So what does this mean? Should we receive the text of scripture literally, and simply accept that no one can see God and live? If that is the case, why then do so many other scriptures encourage us to seek His face?

"Hear my voice when I call, LORD; be merciful to me and answer me. My heart says of you, "Seek his face!" Your face, LORD, I will seek. Do not hide your face from me, do not turn your servant away in anger; you have been my helper. Do not reject me or forsake me, God my Savior. Though my father and mother forsake me, the LORD will receive me." *(Psalm 27:7-10* **NIV)**

"If my people, who are called by my name, will humble themselves and pray and seek my face and turn from their wicked ways, then I will hear from heaven, and I will forgive their sin and will heal their land." (2 Chronicles 7:14 NIV)

"Seek the LORD and his strength, seek his face continually." (1 Chronicles 16:11 KJV)

At the very least, one would have to admit that this appears to be conflicting. In one excerpt, the scripture seems to suggest that we cannot see God's face and live; yet, in so many other references, it very clearly implores that we should seek God's face. Our God is certainly not schizophrenic. Then why are these scriptures seemingly contrary to the statement God made to Moses, declaring that no man can see God's face and live?

The answer is hidden inside The Rock. It was in the cleft of the Rock that Moses was hid. But why was Moses satisfied with that compromise, seeing that even then, he still did not see God's face?

The answer is simple, JESUS IS ENOUGH. Jesus is equal to and greater than all that we will ever need. Jesus is enough and He is that Rock.

> *"...And did all drink the same spiritual drink: for they drank of that spiritual Rock that followed them: and that Rock was Christ." (1 Corinthians 10:4 KJV)*
>
> *"It is the LORD of hosts whom you should regard as holy. And He shall be your fear, and He shall be your dread. Then He shall become a sanctuary; but to both the houses of Israel, a stone to strike and a rock to stumble over, and a snare and a trap for the inhabitants of Jerusalem." (Isaiah 8:13-14 NAS)*

*"Just as it is written, "BEHOLD, I LAY IN ZION **A STONE OF STUMBLING AND A ROCK OF OFFENSE**, AND HE WHO BELIEVES IN HIM WILL NOT BE DISAPPOINTED." (Romans 9:33 NAS)*

So Moses was hidden inside that rock. Dare I imagine, in the spiritual sense, that this rock was Christ? Could this have been a foreshadowing of things to come?

Of course, Moses was actually hid within a literal rock, but imagine with me for a moment. Outside of Christ, we are filthy and insufficient, incomplete, unholy and therefore separated from the presence of our Holy God. But in steps Jesus, who is equal and synonymous with God, being the express image of the living God, we now have access.

> **"Philip said, "Lord, show us the Father and that will be enough for us."**
>
> **"Jesus answered:** *"Don't you know me, Philip, even after I have been among you such a long time? Anyone who has seen me has seen the Father. How can you say, 'Show us the Father'? Don't you believe that I am in the Father, and that the Father is in me? The words I say to you I do not speak on my own authority. Rather, it is the Father, living in me, who is doing his work. Believe me when I say that I am in the Father and the Father is in me; or at least believe on the evidence of the works themselves. Very truly I tell you, whoever believes in me will do the works I have been doing, and they will do even greater things than these, because I am going to the Father. And I will do whatever you ask in my name, so that the Father may be glorified in the Son. You may ask me for anything in my name, and I will do it.""* **(John 14:8-14 NIV)** *JESUS IS ENOUGH!!!*

In this revelation we should understand that we must therefore die to self before we can see God. No one can see God and live, because to see God is to die to self and allow the life of Christ to live within us. To see God means that we have allowed the grace of Christ, who is eternal, to clothe us in the presence of

His glory. We can only see God when we gain access to Him through The Rock. We can only see God when we recognize our own insufficiency and hide ourselves amidst the comfort of His mercy. We only see God when we lose focus of our own self-righteousness and recognize that we are only made pure through the grace of Jesus Christ. God's presence is a privilege, so is the revelation of His identity.

The eyes of the proud will be perpetually blind, until humility allows such eyes to be granted access to God's glory. In all our searching for wisdom and knowledge, amidst our quest for deep insight, we should remember that there is no depth without the presence of God; all other knowledge is shallow and superficial.

CHAPTER 26

<u>SIMPLICITY</u>

It is easier to make lofty and extravagant plans than it is to actually do something simple. Some people get caught up in the planning of complicated endeavours that sound impressive, yet are never completed. Many of those extravagant plans failed because the planner was more in love with the theory than the application of the assignment. It is therefore in the doing of a thing that progress is truly measured.

Sure, sitting down to strategize and plan out your steps can be seen as progressive. The necessity of planning and having a good strategy was previously outlined, and it is certainly very important. However, strategy without the eventual intent of production can sometimes become deflating. The behaviour of planning alone without any intention of execution is practised in vain. Some of us place a greater desire in sounding impressive over being productive. But more impressive than lofty plans are sustaining characteristics, such as commitment, effort and consistency. Tomorrow cannot create a reality of excellence if today is spent dreaming about tomorrow. Greatness is achieved by being consistent in multiple acts of simplicity. Dreams without productivity aren't dreams, but instead only fantasies.

"For our boast is this, the testimony of our conscience, that we behaved in the world with simplicity and godly sincerity, not by earthly wisdom but by the grace of God, and supremely so toward you." (2 Corinthians 1:12 ESV)

Living the simple life doesn't necessarily mean that we shouldn't or cannot aspire to achieve great things. Instead, it speaks more to the motive of our endeavour rather than the stature of our accomplishments. We should ensure that our focus isn't to devise plans in order to invite the praise of man. It seems obvious in its suggestion, but it is quite easy to become enamoured by the approval of our peers; so much so that we can become shortsighted and begin to pursue temporal accolades, instead of resting in the peace that is obtained by simply doing God's will.

If you have a dream, work towards it daily. Learn the art of baby-steps. Like a spider who builds a web, slowly but surely you'll accomplish the task. Nothing of sustaining value is ever achieved through happenstance. Seeds of mediocrity will never produce the fruit of excellence.

CHAPTER 27

<u>LIFE LESSONS 101</u>

Of course, life has numerous lessons to teach us, and by no means am I professing to be an expert on the subject of life. Like you, I am most definitely imperfect and still learning, still making some mistakes along the way and trying my very best each day to ensure that my mistakes don't become habitual or recurring without remedy. During some of those mistakes, I did eventually learn that there are at least three fundamental truths about this journey of life. I call them Life Lessons. In the midst of a very complex world, I've found that these 3 key guidelines stand true with crystal clear simplicity.

LESSON 1: Always make a plan, because just "winging it" might be fine for your PlayStation and Xbox game consoles, but in real life we only get one go at it, and life has no reset buttons. So write the vision and make it plain. Once you've made a plan, have the courage to start something.

LESSON 2: Always have a *Plan B*, because life happens, and when it does, we aren't always prepared for it. Things simply don't always line up exactly how we originally planned.

LESSON 3: Learn sooner than later that your lesson 3 should have been your lesson 1, because lesson 3 is simple, yet a necessary component to your success. In life, it truly does not matter what your Plan A or Plan B may be, for a certainty you are still destined to experience some trouble.

No matter how intricate and well calculated our life plans may be, life will inevitably bring you road blocks and detours; your only security will rest on who your tour guide is on this journey. If you are your own guide, life is going to get rougher and it's going to get tougher. There are some places in life that you haven't been, and when you do get there, you'll discover that your limited knowledge may leave you lost, frustrated and confused. However, if your tour guide is he who built the road map, your chance of success is significantly more optimistic.

Most definitively, *the summarizing truth of Lesson 3 is*: All the ways of man are feeble at best, and destined for error. We are full of flaws and imperfection. On our own we are lost and incomplete. But, *"On Christ the solid rock I stand, all other ground is sinking sand."* Therefore, in life, make sure that your tour guide isn't yourself. Ensure that your guide sees far beyond where your eyes can reach.

CHAPTER 28

TAMING THE BEAST

Fire is an interesting thing, used in so many productive ways. We use fire to purify and to prepare our nourishment. The steam engines of the past were given their names because of the use of steam to propel the movement of the trains. In that context, fire is progressive, it's advancing, and it is productive. But without containment of that coal fire, without controlling its flames, that same fire can be destructive, dangerous and life threatening. On that train, the same fire without boundaries would not only jeopardize the train's progress, it could potentially consume the vessel completely.

Our vessel is very much like that train. We are like travelling locomotives on course to a specific destination, while making our way through a foreign land. Because the land is not our own, we often have to travel through regions occupied by the enemy. We must remain focused and try our best to ensure that we do not stop by the wayside. Our adversary is cunning and desires to push us off course; we must therefore remain on task and get to our destination, arriving whole and intact.

We cannot allow our passion to overwhelm us if we are intending on reaching our goal. Uncontrolled passion leads to burnout and stagnation. Wild fire in any capacity is unpredictable. Humans are passionate beings. We often make decisions based on our emotions and intuitions. We are often led by the fire within instead of by logical reasoning. From the most educated to the most unlearned individual, none of us is exempt from the burn of the internal fire. That fire will either become a productive tool to use for something progressive, or if we aren't careful, it can become something dangerous that threatens the momentum of our purpose. The choice is ours.

We all have passion, for something, at some point in our lives. This passion that resides within, if not placed under control, can become like a wild beast within us. Whether that passion is anger, lust of physical intimacy, the ugly beast of pride, or the pacifying effect of an addictive substance, there is a beast that threatens to rise up within us and run wild in a rage of destruction. The carnal man is that beast. We must therefore put that beast under subjection every day. It can consume us, it can kill purpose and it can harm those that are closest to us. We must therefore learn to tame that beast.

This is why we die daily. The carnal man is constantly at war with the divine purpose within us. God has instilled destiny in each life, but that destiny is buried in the form of potential. Therefore, we will only eat of its fruit if we cultivate the seed that was planted inside of us. After the seed is buried it must still be watered and given the right exposure of light in order to germinate. God's word is that light.

"Your word is a lamp to guide my feet and a light for my path." (Psalm 119:105 NLT)

The daily outpouring of worship and prayer is equivalent to the process of precipitation that produces the water that is needed to feed the roots of our purpose.

"As a deer pants for flowing streams, so pants my soul for you, O God. My soul thirsts for God, for the living God. When shall I come and appear before God?" *(Psalm 42:1-2 ESV)*

The deer, as all living creatures, vehemently searches for water because it recognizes that the water is an essential source of its survival. David declared, with the same spirit of desperation and urgency that the deer seeks to quench its thirst, his soul longs for and searches daily for the living God. Without that source, his soul would faint. Without that source, David recognized that his spiritual life would wither away and surely die.

The beast must therefore be tamed and subjugated so that the spirit man may live instead. Whatever is being fed within us is the creature that will ultimately grow. We can't continue to feed our lusts and yet expect that there will be consistent manifestations of spiritual growth. The beast must be tamed and starved, and ultimately crucified, so that the spirit may live and have room to develop within us. But if we are to starve the beast within us, we must therefore simultaneously feed the spirit.

> *"But he knows where I am going. And when he tests me, I will come out as pure as gold. For I have stayed on God's paths; I have followed his ways and not turned aside. I have not departed from his commands, but have treasured his words more than daily food." (Job 23: 10-12 NLT)*

Job understood the importance of the word of God. To Job, God's word was more necessary to him than his daily consumption of food. That's quite a deep statement. That's quite a bold statement of reliance upon the word of God; not only when it is convenient, but instead as daily intake that's necessary for survival. Perhaps this is why God trusted Job with such severe trials. Perhaps God knew that the substance within Job, the word that he daily fed upon, was enough to sustain him even amidst earth-shattering realities.

Job faced no simple ordeal. His cattle, which would be considered as a means of currency and livelihood at that time, were taken from him. The material possessions that he worked for many years to obtain were quickly snatched from him, seemingly without reason and without explanation. If that wasn't enough, his children, which were without a doubt far more cherished than his possessions, were also snatched from him without reason and without explanation.

Surely that would have been enough to shake the faith of many of us. Surely the testing and trials would end there, right? But they didn't. Even amidst such deep despair, Job still had to deal with the affliction of ailment in his body. Sores and boils consumed his flesh to the severity that his appearance was altered, so much so that his friends could barely recognize him at first when they came to visit him.

This was no regular illness. Job was in pain day and night; he was suffering in continuous agony. In this state of hopelessness, Job couldn't even find solace in the support of a loving wife; because even she turned against him and offered him unwise counsel. She was resolved in the belief that Job was undoubtedly receiving severe punishment that was sent from the Lord. Job's wife was utterly convinced that Job was in a hopeless situation and that he should consequently resort to cursing God and hope that His final judgment upon Job would be death.

Wow, that's such a harsh reality to face. Your finances are taken from you, your children have recently all died, your friends are accusing you of being an unjust man who is deserving of these afflictions; which they say is God's punishment upon you, and your loving wife is telling you that death is your best option. Not a pretty picture to say the least. Yet, amidst all of that, amidst all of such hopelessness, Job still had hope in God's word. The word of the Lord to Job had become more important than his food; so even when his body, finance, and family were being afflicted, and his friends condemned him, his *faith* still remained intact.

The consumption of the Word is for the fortifying of our faith, so that we may be able to stand during our moments of testing. God's voice is not always present, sometimes God remains silent and allows us to demonstrate the evidence of the confidence that He has in our integrity. God's silence does not mean his absence. Therefore, even within the silence of dark situations, we must stay the course and allow His faithfulness to outlast our circumstance.

CHAPTER 29

THE HORIZON OF DESTINY

There is a point along the road of purpose where suddenly almost everything becomes clear. As you approach the horizon of your destiny, the dark clouds of uncertainty begin to dissipate. At this juncture, there is an alignment of purposeful individuals in your life. But amidst this divine orchestration there are choices that must be made. We are often two steps away from destiny with one leg amidst the valley of indecision. The atmospheric change occurs when we resolve to choose destiny over the cyclical re-occurrence of stagnation. Therefore, with a thundering blow, there is now a wind of progress in the air. I can see clearly now; I choose life, I choose destiny. I choose to manifest the purpose that has been burning internally.

It is here, on the cusp of that horizon that we must continue to fan the flames of the passion we possess for our purpose; this ensures that we do not lose steam in the final push towards manifesting our destiny. Here we will face more than criticism and opposition. We will once again face the doubts of our own mind, reminding us of all our failures and rehearsing in our memory all previous moments of defeat. We must therefore face ourselves and determine that our future is not determined by our past, nor will past mistakes cause us to become crippled in the face of promise. It is hard to receive a promise that has been seemingly snatched from our grasp numerous times before.

This is why the battle becomes a war of the mind. It becomes a battle with self-perception. It is a continuous struggle amongst the personifications of who we think we are, who we use to be, and who God has created us to become. The struggle ends when we begin to believe what God says about us. There is peace in accepting the identity that God has created us to be.

We have been shaped and defined by an entire world. That world is filled with individuals who suffer from identity crisis, who attempt to live vicariously through the lives of others because they haven't figured out exactly who they should become. There are individuals around you that have tried to paint their image upon the canvas of your identity. They tell you who you are and what you cannot become. They tell you what your limitations should be, and they attempt to outline the boundaries around you that limit your potential. But quite often, these are people who have lived a life of fear and condemnation within their own lives, and they are trying to instill that negative perception upon you; because as we know, misery loves company in the valley of defeat.

But on the horizon of destiny you must pull away from all of that false identity, and shake away from that negative perception. You must make a decision to either become the person others want you to be, or choose to walk in the identity of God's design. There is greatness inside of you, and you should be unapologetic about manifesting that identity. You are standing at the doorsteps of promise; from this vantage point, you now have clear sight of the garden of possibilities. The harvest is ripe with unlimited potential, but you must believe in the plan that God has ordained for your life.

You must accept the calling that is on your life and no longer be afraid to live in excellence. You can no longer be *normal*. You can no longer embrace mediocrity; it is not a part of your DNA. You are made by divine artistry. God's masterpiece was never created to be hidden under the covers of mediocrity. Arise, shine! Be bright, be bold and be audacious! Continually fan the flames of your purpose, and let it perpetually burn. Let it push you towards an overflow of prominence.

Be contagious in your existence. You are not here by happenstance. Be intentional in your interactions, your relationships matter and each connection comes with a consequence. Each decision that we make staggers a repercussion that has some effect to the path of our purpose, either good or bad. We are products of our decisions and no one can deny us of our destiny unless we allow it.

It is time to rise and shine amidst the light that has come to illuminate the brilliance of your purpose. Upon this horizon is where you must grab a hold of destiny and run militantly without looking back. You haven't faced your last giant, nor have you encountered your last moment of defeat; but if you trust in the Lord, who is your General, He promises to deliver a victorious ending to a war that has already been won.

You are victorious. You are a conqueror. Walk in purpose. Be passionate in your pursuit of greatness. Shun the temptation to exist amidst camouflaged identities. You insult the strength of your purpose when you attempt to live in the emulation of someone else. No one can ever beat you at being you. So do just that, be you. In doing so, do it gallantly and without apology.

The pressure and climate of your trials have come to bring clarity to the cloudy situations of your life, while God turns your dark moments into channels of light for His glory. Your value won't be truly seen until you have been pressed and shaken, yet without being completely broken. Your trials come to chisel you and mould you into a greater you. The darkness will be made light before you and the high places will be brought down. That diamond in the rough has now been polished and fitted, and ready for presentation. Your value will shine as you unlock the true potential within you.

> *"I will lead the blind by ways they have not known, along unfamiliar paths I will guide them; I will turn the darkness into light before them and make the rough places smooth. These are the things I will do; I will not forsake them." (Isaiah 42:16 NIV)*

Now that you have found purpose, what will you accomplish with it? Now that you have found the path of destiny, will you continue upon it? Don't bury the gift that was created to be a healing to the world. You hold the remedy within you to a dying world. Don't allow the past to hold you captive. This is the dawning of a new season in your life, a season of progress and purpose. Keep moving forward, your destiny awaits you!

You have separated yourself from those who desire to keep you stagnant. You have created within your lifestyle sustaining habits of success. You have tapped into the potential of your purpose and a passionate desire has been ignited. The world has never seen the brilliance that you have to offer. They are waiting to receive what you have within you. So now and always, ensure that you live your life with a passionate pursuit of purpose. Be influential and effectual in all that you do.

> *"A final word: Be strong in the Lord and in his mighty power. Put on all of God's armor so that you will be able to stand firm against all strategies of the devil." (Ephesians 6:10-11 NLT)*

If you've come across the pages of this book and you find yourself to be standing outside of a relationship with the Lord Jesus Christ, please take this opportunity as an invitation to receive of His saving grace into your life. *"For God so loved the world that He gave His only begotten Son, that whoever believes in Him should not perish but have everlasting life." (John 3:16 NKJV)*

"*Now unto him that is able to keep you from falling, and to present you faultless before the presence of his glory with exceeding joy, to the only wise God our Saviour, be glory and majesty, dominion and power, both now and ever. Amen.*"
(Jude, verse 24-25 KJV)

Printed in the United States
By Bookmasters